Ready, Aim Impact!

Ready, Aim, Impact!

The Expert Insights System for Entrepreneurial Success

Foreword by Jim Stovall,
Best-Selling Author of *The Ultimate Gift*

Featured Experts:
Michael E. Gerber, Dr. Cathy Greenberg,
Dr. Relly Nadler, Kendall SummerHawk,
Christian Mickelsen, Dr. Sherry Buffington,
Viki Winterton, Tsufit, James Malinchak,
Dr. Sharon Melnick, Lisa Bloom,
Michael Charest

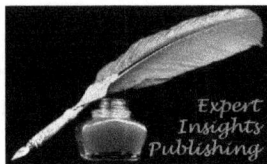

*Expert
Insights
Publishing*

Ready, Aim, Impact!
The Expert Insights System for Entrepreneurial Success
©2011 by Viki Winterton

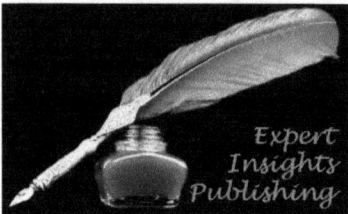

Expert Insights Publishing
1001 East WT Harris Blvd #247
Charlotte, NC 28213

ISBN:978-0-9837379-0-2

Printed Green in the United States of America by Greyden Press
Cover Design: Terry Z
Edited by: Chris Wallace
Interviews: Donna Amos, Stacey Chadwell, Toni Reece, Callan Rush, and Viki Winterton

15 14 13 12 11   1 2 3 4 5

A portion of the proceeds from the sale of this book will be donated to world literacy, One Laptop Per Child.

To my dearest Terry Z and all
entrepreneurial souls who make an impact
on this world each moment through
your contribution of
unique talents and creative spirit.
Namaste.

Table of Contents

Michael E. Gerber

"With the E-Myth, Michael E. Gerber has created the seminal business development system for the small business owner. Now, with The Dreaming Room, he is offering us the next level—the opportunity to awaken the entrepreneur deep within us and dream bigger than we ever have before. When I heard I could spend three days with Michael E. Gerber and receive personal coaching from the world's number one small business guru, I literally jumped at the chance. I experienced a total transformation that has had an immediate and explosive effect on my business. I implore you . . . please . . . don't walk, don't run, but sprint to The Dreaming Room. You and your business will never be the same."
—**Michael Port,** Best-Selling Author of *Book Yourself Solid*

Dr. Cathy Greenberg

"Cathy Greenberg is one of the most creative and refreshing thinkers in our field. Dr. Greenberg's unique background gives her an 'anthropologist's view' of organizations and their leaders. She is able to combine both scientific objectivity and passion in her work. She is one of the few professionals in our field that can be effectively practical and idealistic at the same time. Cathy is also unique in that she has both a deep understanding of big business and ongoing commitment to worthwhile human services organizations. She is a frequent volunteer and is almost always willing to pitch in for a good cause. In my twenty-six years of consulting, I have seen 'the good, the bad, and the ugly.' I am proud that Cathy and I are friends, colleagues, co-authors, and fellow professionals."
—**Dr. Marshall Goldsmith,** Best-Selling Author and World Leadership Authority

Dr. Relly Nadler

"Relly Nadler, one of the world's foremost executive coaches, provides the reader with detailed and easy-to-use practices to make you and your leaders superstars. One of the most valuable leadership books available!"
—**Jeffrey E. Auerbach, Ph.D.,** President, College of Executive Coaching, Author of *Personal and Executive Coaching*

"If you're looking for the plays and strategies to raise emotional intelligence, this is the handbook."
—**Jack Canfield,** Co-Creator of *Chicken Soup for the Soul*, Co-Author of *The Success Principle*™

"Reldan S. Nadler . . . delivers. He offers keys to improving our leadership potential as well. Relly's work is smart, practical, and easy to use. He delivers a solid and comprehensive presentation of emotional intelligence in a manner that suits the reading audience that is looking for clear information quickly. His assessments, evaluations, and inventories point clearly to behaviors worth noting."
—**David J. Mahoney, Ph.D.,** *Psychologist, Consultant, Executive Coach*

Kendall SummerHawk

"My biggest challenges before I started working with Kendall were not knowing how to charge what I felt like I was worth, how to transform my outdated coaching model, how to effectively market to my clients so they would be compelled to work with me, and how to develop tools for exploring the internal side of money challenges. As a result of working with Kendall in her Money Breakthrough Method Coach Training Program, I now have a handle on all of that. I have focused my area of work, attracted ideal clients, and have become much better at communicating my value. I am so grateful I made the investment in myself, and that I did it in one of Kendall's programs."
—**Leslie Cunningham,** Creator of Financial Dating Wealth™

Christian Mickelsen

"Christian has extensive experience as a small business coach and life coach. He has been seen in Forbes, MSN, Yahoo Finance *and* The Boston Globe. *He spent two years on the board of directors of the International Association of Coaching. He has developed numerous support programs to help coaches become financially successful. Christian was my business coach for a full year. He was instrumental in getting my Marketing Action groups off the ground a few years ago. Christian used a free session with me to get me as a client. It definitely worked.* He's perfected this methodology."
—**Robert Middleton,** Action Plan Marketing

Dr. Sherry Buffington

"The best part of waking up these past ten years has not been Maxwell House coffee; it has been the addition of three exquisite tools from Dr. Sherry Buffington allowing me to strengthen my Executive and Personal Performance Coaching business with amazing clients who achieve exceptional results.

Dr. Sherry Buffington is a psychologist, author, and trainer who is deeply beloved and respected for her graciousness, brilliance, creativity, generosity, and the nonstop, sustainable results people experience from the cutting-edge tools she has created. She makes a mammoth difference in others' lives. Thousands of people have recovered their authentic selves, gotten back their healthy lives, restored their relationships, grabbed back their sanity, found their self confidence, or recovered their physical health as a result of her work."
—**Jill Pickett,** Executive & Personal Performance Coach

Viki Winterton

"I am mightily impressed with Viki's dedication and creativity in launching a powerful organization like The Coach Exchange. Her caring and support is evident in the manner in which she brings coaches together (like The Coaches' Edge Extravaganza). It's clear that Viki understands and values integrity, communication, and relationships, and is a master at demonstrating excellence in all three of those key areas of business."
—**Schelli Whitehouse,** Pegasus UnLimited Possibilities, Inc.

"Many thanks for your ongoing harvesting of the collective intelligence of the community. You're having a tangible impact with the tireless work you're doing."
—**Lloyd Raines, MCC,** Principal, Integral Focus

Tsufit

"Tsufit's Step Into the Spotlight *is a must-read for every aspiring or seasoned professional. She reveals her secrets for success with mind-blowing strategies and networking techniques that will take everyone's career to a new level. Tsufit's writing style makes* Step Into the Spotlight *a pleasurable read. Because of her proven methods, I will be using several tactics for my career."*
—**Les Brown,** Internationally Renowned Motivational Speaker

James Malinchak

"James Malinchak has given you the tools to unlock some of the closed doors of the business world. His strategies could be the key to your success!"
—**Joe Theismann,** ESPN Football Analyst, Former Super Bowl Champion, All-Pro Quarterback of the Washington Redskins

"If you're ready to WOW your audience and take them to new heights of success, love, and happiness, then you need to hear my friend James Malinchak!"
—**Mark Victor Hansen,** Co-Creator of the Number One Best-Selling Book Series _Chicken Soup for the Soul_

Dr. Sharon Melnick

"I have turbo-charged my professional life. I let go of trying to get other people's approval and now focus on what's best for the organization. I contribute more, and my self-evaluation is positive, not negative. Its like I was driving a clunky car that doesn't turn well, and now I've stepped into a Porsche; the performance is just superior. I have been pulled aside for recognition by colleagues and complimented by the president of my organization. I have been able to tee up a more meaningful role in my organization and the next stage of my career. I eliminated behaviors that would have hurt my professional advancement and now act consistent with my nomination to a position of greater leadership.

Sharon's portfolio of techniques is powerful . . . I was skeptical when she said I could make changes quickly, after I had tried for so long to make improvements based on others' techniques. What we discussed were things I had heard about and known intellectually, but Sharon was able to break through to me emotionally and help me find and identify the internal 'glass wall' that had been holding me back. Now I am confident and act with clarity and purpose. It's been unbelievable and worth every penny—even much more!"
—**Mark M.,** NYSERDA

Lisa Bloom

"It is one of the most satisfying things I've done, since it was the fulfillment of a dream, and I didn't think I would ever be able to manage it . . . Lisa did a GREAT job in supporting this life goal. Lisa was patient, inventive, thoughtful, and caring in helping me get to a better place and manage a sensitive and important relationship. Thank you for being such a good coach . . . You are a treasure."
—**Ann Berzak,** VP Marketing, CA, USA

Michael Charest

"And then there's Michael the human being—what a huge heart and generous, fun spirit. He will become your boldest uplifting champion. He'll ask the right questions to get you to cut to the chase and focus on what you need to do for real business growth. He'll help you explicitly lay out the steps and go for it.

I encourage everyone—new and veteran business owners—to come enjoy laughing with Michael, and gain eye-opening new value for your business and the quality of your life."
—**Marian Baker,** Master Certified Coach, Author, WakeUpInspired.com

"Michael's 'heartfelt business' philosophy totally spiced up my life. His warm common sense approach combined with business fortitude empowered me to TOTALLY grow my business. What I used to earn in ONE YEAR I earned in the last TWO MONTHS . . . If you want to totally grow your business and your life, give Michael a call."
—**Chere Bork,** Savor Your Life Today! www.cherecoach.com

Jim Stovall: *The Ultimate Gift*

When I was a young man, I had a goal to become an all-American football player and to play for the Dallas Cowboys in the NFL. That was the plan for my life, and I was well on my way to doing just that when during a routine physical to go play a season of ball, I was diagnosed with a condition that would and did result in me losing my eyesight. It may interest you to know that at that time and to this very day there has never been a blind player on the Dallas Cowboys' team, so I realized I was going to have to do something else.

I finished my athletic career as an Olympic weightlifter and enjoyed that experience, and then I started my business career and had to learn other ways of doing things. Every obstacle is an opportunity to learn a new way of doing something, and my obstacle is no greater or lesser than yours or any of the people you work with. An obstacle is nothing more or less than the biggest thing it takes to keep us from where we want to be; getting over that obstacle is not a matter of dealing with the obstacle itself, it's a matter of grasping a bigger goal on the other side.

If I were to ask if you could climb a two-story brick wall and crawl into a window, you'd most likely tell me, "Probably not." If I told you your youngest child is in there and you've got five minutes before they perish in a fire, you'd probably get it done. I haven't changed the obstacle, I've changed the goal on the other side.

So anytime someone is bogged down by an obstacle, don't mess with the obstacle, don't tell them it's not a big deal, don't tell them they've got to overcome. Don't tell them any of that stuff. Just make the goal big enough and they'll get over it. When the dream is big enough, the facts simply don't count anymore.

As I said, I was young—twenty-nine years old—and had never met a blind person. I didn't have a clue what I was going to do with the rest of my life. The only plan I could come up with at that point was to move into a little nine-by-twelve-foot room in the back of my house. In my little room I had a radio, a telephone, and a tape recorder; that was my whole world at age twenty-nine. I fully intended to never walk out of that room again. You will never meet a more helpless, hopeless person than I was then.

I stayed in that room month after month, and finally, with a lot of support and encouragement, I decided to leave my little room. I wasn't coming out of there to build a television network, to write a best-selling book, to make movies, to speak to a million people a year in arena events, or to make millions of dollars; the first thing I decided to do was to walk fifty-two feet to my mailbox. That was the hardest thing I've ever done in my life thus far.

The anxiety level as I reached the mailbox, drenched with sweat, would be difficult to describe to you. As I reached out my hand and touched that mailbox, my foot touched the curb there right at the edge of my street. Even though I had lived in that house on that street for over a decade, I discovered something there that I had never realized during the years I'd had my eyesight; I realized that if I could get to that curb and make it those fifty-two feet, then maybe other things were possible in my life, and I discovered right then and there that I lived on a magic street. The street I lived on was connected to another street, which intersected with still another, and that street would take me anywhere in the world I wanted to go; it did, and it still does.

I found myself sitting in that little room that I thought I would never leave, and when the fear of not trying overcomes the fear of failure, then we get up and move. I sat there day after day after day, and I realized that if I didn't do something, I was going to die in that little room. Whatever was out there in the big scary world that I was afraid of couldn't be a whole lot worse than spending the rest of my life in that little room. I thought, *People who commit crimes go to the penitentiary and live in places like this—why am I here?*

So I walked out of there, and a little at a time, the world opened up for me. It's still difficult. I don't ever want people to think that I jumped over that hurdle and suddenly life became shady and downhill and wonderful all the time. There are still challenges and obstacles, and in a sense that's what makes it great, that's what makes it fun, and that's why there's always room at the top.

Great things happen. My obstacle has never changed. I'm still as totally blind today as I was those years ago, but my whole world changed because somehow, in the process of losing my sight, I was able to capture a new vision of who I could be. I had to experience blindness to gain a new vision, but I can honestly say that it was worth it. I've lived my life without sight, and I've lived my life without vision, and vision is certainly a more valuable commodity. As precious as sight is, vision is worth more.

I'm a huge baseball fan, and I am still convinced I could go to the World Series being totally blind and that I could get a hit in a Major League Baseball game if they'd let me have as many strikes as I want. Let me stand there until I finally hit it, and eventually I'll get a hit.

In baseball you only get three strikes; in life, it's not over until you say it's over—you can keep doing anything you want to do. To me, failure doesn't matter. I've had the tremendous advantage of seeing the bottom. I've been broke and blind and suicidal and stuck in a little room I thought I'd never get out of. From there, there's nowhere to go but up—it's all great and wonderful. What else is going to happen to me?

I wrote a line for *The Ultimate Gift,* and James Garner delivered it in the movie when he lost everything. He said, "I've lost everything two or three times; it's the perfect place to start." It's true—what a great opportunity.

There's a quote I love that was spoken by a general in World War II. He was totally surrounded. Patton was trying to relieve him but couldn't get there for a day or two. They asked him if he was going to surrender because he was totally surrounded. His response was, "No, we're not going to surrender. We have the tremendous advantage of being able to address the enemy in any direction."

That's the way life is—when you've got nothing to lose, you've got absolutely everything to gain. There are a whole lot of people holding on to mediocrity, and they're afraid to let go of it because they're afraid they're going to lose what they do have. The only thing they're risking is everything in the world they could gain.

As a best-selling author, I am embarrassed to say that prior to losing my sight, I don't know that I ever read a whole book cover to cover. I read enough to get through school, but after losing my sight twenty years ago, I discovered the National Library for the Blind which makes audio books available to blind people on special recordings. I helped develop a high-speed player that would play the recordings faster, so I can listen to books now at seven hundred or eight hundred words a minute. Through that process I am able to read a book every day.

There has not been a day since 1988 when I haven't read a whole book cover to cover including today, and that has literally altered my life in amazing ways. I discovered that while I didn't have a lot of powerful friends and mentors and those types of resources to get me out of that at that point in time (though there were a few people who came around me who made a difference), the best resource I had was access to the best and brightest and most significant minds that had ever lived available to me anytime, any day, any hour; all I had to do was read a book.

People always ask, "How do you become a writer?" I always tell them, "You have to become a reader before you become a writer." That's what changed my life.

To find inspiration, I started learning from everyone. Ralph Waldo Emerson once said, "Every man I meet is in some way my superior." There is always something of value to be gleaned from learning from the wisdom of others. That is why I recommend you read *Ready, Aim Impact!* today. Every expert in this outstanding book has something valuable to teach us.

Jim Stovall

—Best-Selling Author of 15 books,
—President of the Emmy-Award Winning Narrative Television Network
—Champion Olympic Weightlifter
—International Humanitarian of the Year, Joining Jimmy Carter, Nancy Reagan, and Mother Teresa as Recipients of This Honor

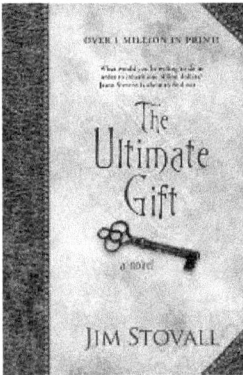

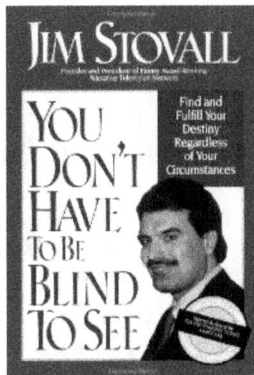

"Jim Stovall is one of the most extraordinary men of our era."
—Steve Forbes, President and CEO of *Forbes* Magazine

We live in the most confusing climate of our era when even "tried and true" client attraction and retention methods are just not working. Some of the best marketers are finding it challenging to attract the audience who may have flocked to them just a few short months ago. We see fees dropping, entrepreneurs offering more for less, and new slants on old business models aren't cutting it anymore. Along with these challenges comes increased difficulty as we strive to form meaningful connections in the midst of a technology-driven society.

We must face the reality that yesterday's solutions won't solve today's problems. To be successful in reaching out, maintaining relationships, generating new business, and remaining competitive in our industry, we must identify a new approach.

In this indispensable resource, top visionaries and experts share their success secrets, proven formulas, and the defining moments that have shaped their lives and careers. A wealth of information is delivered within these exclusive interviews for the purpose of guiding you on your own journey to success.

You have a vision for what you hope your business—your contribution to the world—will be. But the road to get there often seems winding, uneven, and filled with pitfalls. Sit back, take a deep breath, and allow each of these experts to share with you about their own personal journey. Explore the dedication it required, which processes proved successful, where it led them, and what they learned along the way. Each conversation contained in these pages is empowering, inspiring, and priceless, and you will find yourself in the pages of these interviews and in these accounts of occupational achievement and personal triumph.

Let go of your fears, try something new, and step into a promising future, allowing these success stories to guide you along the way.

> "There are a whole lot of people holding on to mediocrity, and they're afraid to let go of it because they're afraid they're going to lose what they do have. The only thing they're risking is everything in the world they could gain . . . Ralph Waldo Emerson once said, 'Every man I meet is in some way my superior.' There is always something of value to be gleaned from learning from the wisdom of others . . . Every expert in this outstanding book has something valuable to teach us." (Jim Stovall)

Chapter 1

Why Entrepreneurs Fail
Michael E. Gerber

Chapter 1
Why Entrepreneurs Fail
Michael E. Gerber

Michael E. Gerber is the founder of Michael E. Gerber Companies, a coaching, training, and education firm he created in 1977 to transform the development of small businesses worldwide. Now approaching his 32nd year, Michael's extraordinary work has achieved stunning results by transforming more than 65,000 businesses in over 145 countries. His book, *The E-Myth Revisited*, has been translated into twenty-nine languages and has been used in 118 universities throughout the world.

Michael has founded eleven new ventures in the last four years. Michael lives with his wife, Luz Delia, in Carlsbad, California, where they are intentionally and joyously pursuing their shared vision for "transforming the world one business at a time."

I: I understand that Dave Ramsey, Robert Kiyosaki, Jack Canfield, and Tim Ferriss all recommend your *New York Times* best seller, *The E-Myth Revisited*. What is the E-Myth?

MG: The E-Myth is the entrepreneurial myth. Essentially, it is the cause for the vast majority of small businesses going out of business on a regular basis. The entrepreneurial myth means that the people who start businesses aren't really the entrepreneurs we think they are, but rather what I've come to call "technicians suffering from an entrepreneurial seizure."

They create a job for themselves rather than creating a business that can operate without them. They don't create a business that's scalable—that has its own form, substance, and systems that operate independent of the founder or owner.

I: Why do entrepreneurs fail?

MG: Entrepreneurs fail for all sorts of reasons, but true entrepreneurs fail simply because the timing of what they've invented isn't right, the capital isn't available, or they missed the point in the starting of their venture. The fact is that the people you think of as entrepreneurs aren't really entrepreneurs at all.

Entrepreneurs in the main succeed or fail abruptly because they always start something that's significantly bigger than anything they've ever done before—significantly different than anything anyone has ever done before—and because of that, they're playing in a very solitary and unusual game.

On the other hand, all of the other guys who start companies aren't entrepreneurs at all. As I said earlier, they're technicians suffering from an entrepreneurial seizure; they create a job for themselves and then find that they're working for a lunatic—themselves. They get busy doing what they know how to do but fail to do all of the things they absolutely must *learn* how to do in order to build a business that really works.

I: You started The Dreaming Room at the end of 2005, which is a two-and-a-half-day intensive. From your experiences with The Dreaming Room, you wrote *Awakening the Entrepreneur Within.* What is The Dreaming Room, and what happened that inspired the "awakening" book?

MG: The Dreaming Room is what I call an entrepreneurial incubator; it's not an incubator for the business per se, but an incubator of the entrepreneurial personality.

In my book, *Awakening the Entrepreneur Within: How Ordinary People Can Create Extraordinary Companies* without any experience to guide them, I essentially describe or define what an entrepreneur is in a way that has never been defined before. I refer to the four personalities of an entrepreneur that are critical if anything of substance—anything of value—is going to be created.

I: Can a technician be transformed into the kind of entrepreneur that is needed to run these businesses?

MG: The technician, first of all, has to understand that it's not knowing *how* to do the work in your business that's going to make you successful, it's knowing how to *convert* that work into an intelligent system that you can then delegate to others and utilize to produce the result your company has been created to produce.

These four entrepreneurial personalities are critical if the technician in us is going to give way to the entrepreneur within us. Those four personalities are the **dreamer**, the **thinker**, the **storyteller**, and the **leader**.

The Four Entrepreneurial Personalities

1. The Dreamer: *The dreamer has a dream*—a picture of a great result. The dreamer sets out to create a great result. Martin Luther King—while not an entrepreneur but certainly a dreamer—said very simply and straightforwardly, "I have a dream."

The truth is, most entrepreneurs have a dream. Walt Disney had a dream. Michael Dell of Dell computers had a dream. Steve Jobs had a dream. These true entrepreneurs—true creators—certainly and absolutely had dreams that were bigger than life, and they pursued them with everything they had. But a dream is not enough.

2. The Thinker: *The thinker has a vision* for how that great result is going to be produced. That business model will enable that great result to be manifested in the world.

In our particular case, we started in 1977 with what was then called the Michael Thomas Corporation. I was Michael and the other guy was Thomas. I had a *dream* and I had a *vision*. My dream was to transform the state of small business worldwide. My *vision* was to invent the McDonald's of small business consulting. I knew that the key to being able to transform the state of small business worldwide was to do with small business consulting exactly what Ray Kroc did at McDonald's; we needed to transform the state of small business by developing a turnkey system that could be delivered absolutely every single time without fail.

3. The Storyteller: *The storyteller has a purpose.* Entrepreneurs who don't tell stories cannot awaken the energy that's absolutely essential if a business is going to thrive. Every entrepreneur must have a purpose, and the purpose overrides everything else. Our purpose was that no one would ever have to start a small business and fail. Now understand that statistics show that 90%—nine out of ten—of all new businesses will be out of business within five years. It's staggering when you think about it. Given those statistics, one might ask, "What causes those businesses to fail?"

I'll tell you what it is, it's what I said earlier—they're not really entrepreneurs. They go to work, they do what they think needs to be done, but they don't know how to do anything else. The purpose must address someone specific who is going to become the customer for your business, who isn't getting what they need in their life, and who is going to find that your business can provide it for them better than anyone else ever has.

> *"The new entrepreneur truly wants to have a transformational impact on the world. 'The company that I create,' the new entrepreneur would say, 'has to have meaning.'"*

4. The Leader: *The leader has a mission.* The mission is to invent a system through which your *dream*, your *vision*, and your *purpose* can be realized, and that system must be scalable. That means it can grow and deliver what it is you've invented to have a truly transformational impact on the world. That's the fundamental principle of awakening the entrepreneur within, and the fundamental activity we engage in inside The Dreaming Room.

I: That is quite an impressive model. What is the new kind of entrepreneur?

MG: The new entrepreneur is interested in doing something more than simply making money or growing a company. The new entrepreneur truly wants to have a transformational impact on the world. "The company that I create," the new entrepreneur would say, "has to have meaning."

There has to be something beyond simply the business of business. In order to be satisfying, in order to be deliberate, in order to be conscious, I'm convinced that we are going to have to have a profound impact on people and on the circumstances that possess them and that they suffer from. That's what entrepreneurs in this "new age of the new entrepreneurs," as I refer to it, are going to be focusing their attention on.

The perfect example of a new entrepreneur is Muhammad Yunus, the inventor of Grameen Bank micro lending in Bangladesh. He has literally transformed the lives of impoverished women by the millions because of the unique business model that he invented and has continued to grow throughout the world.

It's absolutely stunning what Muhammad Yunus has done. In his book, *Banker to the Poor,* he tells the story of how he did it. It's truly remarkable when you think about it: anyone—literally anyone who has a dream, a vision, a purpose, and a mission—who is truly called to have a profound impact on the conditions that people suffer from in the world can create a great company.

The individual who is called to do that, who is determined to learn how to do that, and who is willing to take the risk to do that is the individual I refer to as the new entrepreneur.

I: They not only want to create a business, they want to make a difference—a big difference.

MG: They want to make a difference and they want to make a difference *differently*. They want to make a difference passionately, and absolutely nothing will keep them from doing it.

I: I like people who are that fired up. I understand you wrote an additional new book based on your reflection on both The Dreaming Room and the "awakening." Can you share a little about your new book, *The E-Myth Enterprise*?

MG: *The E-Myth Enterprise* is a set of stories dealing with four premises. If one were to think of a company as a model, it is a **visual model**, an **emotional model**, a **functional model**, and a **financial model**. It is also visual, emotional, functional, and financial in relationship to its four primary influencers: the **customer**, the **employee**, the **supplier**, and the **lender or investor**. Each of those primary influencers has their own visual, emotional, functional, and financial preferences.

Every entrepreneur who starts a company must start by thinking visually, emotionally, functionally, and financially. When you put those four pieces together and apply them to any company, you will see exactly where that company succeeded in applying those principles, the actions that business took every day to apply them, and where they ignored them. What I'm saying is, ignore them at your own risk.

The E-Myth Enterprise is a series of stories about individuals who *didn't* ignore those principles, but who absolutely pursued them with everything they had. We give a visual, an emotional, a functional, and a financial template for an individual to understand better what I mean by that.

I: How many people have all four of the ingredients you mentioned earlier as being essential to an entrepreneur?

MG: We're all potentially active entrepreneurs. We're all born with an entrepreneur within us. The entrepreneur is nothing other than a creator. Each and every single one of us has a creator within.

Our problem is that part of ourselves is subjugated by our parents, teachers, peers, bosses, friends, associates, etc., to the point where very few of us ever live a truly creative life.

The Dreaming Room is my attempt to awaken that creator inside of each participant. In other words, to me, everyone is stuck where they are. It's not only apparent to me, but I think everyone probably knows to the degree to which they are stuck where they are and can't move beyond that point. We can't move beyond it because our imagination can't see anything beyond it. We feel compelled to be the person we are and to do the things we do.

I'm suggesting that we are significantly more than the person we know, the person we have been, and the habits we've developed over our lifetimes. At the age of seventy-four, I'm saying that every single one of us can rise above it. The way we rise above it is by beginning to *understand our potential* for rising above it, by beginning to *get the experience* of actively pursuing that part of ourselves that lies above it, and by beginning to *feel the movement* within ourselves that causes us to see what's missing in this picture. As we begin to see what's missing, we start to experience a new taste of what living is all about. And as we begin to do that, we ask the question, "So what else could I do, other than what I have done, to give other people the experience that I've just had?"

I: So through The Dreaming Room, you're really bringing the magic within—the creator within—out.

MG: Absolutely. That's what everyone in The Dreaming Room is doing.

"This is not just motivation. This has to happen inside of every single individual. You can't make them do it . . . They have to be hungry for something other than what they have."

It's absolutely astonishing when you experience it. As people walk into The Dreaming Room, they are not able to appreciate what's about to happen. People walk out of The Dreaming Room shocked at how long they've allowed themselves to live without truly tapping into an imagination that was actually a stranger to them. It's like Heinlein's book, *Stranger in a Strange Land*—they're all like strangers living in a strange land, not truly aware of how much creativity resides within them because no one has ever taught them how to tap into it.

That's what we do in The Dreaming Room, it's what we've done at E-Myth worldwide, and it's what we've done in working with the tens of thousands of small business clients—the technicians I mentioned—who have broken businesses simply because they have broken imaginations. They don't truly understand or appreciate how different their business can be and the extraordinary potential that can be accessed simply by beginning to see something they have not seen before.

This is not just motivation. This has to happen *inside* of every single individual. You can't make them do it. You can't simply teach them to do it. They have to be hungry for something other than what they have.

I: You're the number one small business guru, a coach, and you have several coaching programs. What type of person do you work with? I understand that there are going to be entrepreneurs, but who usually comes to you?

MG: We've worked with just about everyone. People ask the question, "Is this appropriate for this particular kind of business or this particular kind of individual?" The answer is no—it's appropriate for anyone who comes and says, "Let's do it."

I don't care who it is, absolutely anyone and everyone who rises to the occasion will begin to discover something inside of themselves that will reveal itself in a way it has never revealed itself before.

CEOs walk in with a company that's dead in its tracks, and they walk out with a company that they never could have imagined they would be leading forward into a completely new role—a new game—to do something they hadn't even conceived of before.

All this happens in a very short period of time. It's absolutely astonishing. When I did my first Dreaming Room in December 2005, I actually hadn't a clue what I was going to do. I just said, "Come dream with me." A blank piece of paper and beginner's mind—that's how we start every Dreaming Room. Not with an idea of what we're going to do, not with a need to pursue some particular vector, not to actively engage with someone I already know inside of myself; no— it's a blank piece of paper.

It's a blank piece of paper regarding your life, your career, your relationships, your company, entrepreneurship, work, creativity, and imagination. That's what is so exquisite about it—it just begins to reveal itself.

If I'm present and if they're present—and if we're passionately convinced that this game we're playing has value to uncover something we have never uncovered before—something magical will happen. It's that magic we're all looking for.

I: Will you share a little about your book, _The Most Successful Small Business in the World_?

MG: It's very difficult to do that in a short interview, but let me say it revolves around the ten principles, and the ten principles simply tell you that there are fundamental realities of a business that is going to soar, is going to grow, and is going to be exponentially successful in what it chooses to do.

The _Most Successful Small Business in the World_ essentially says that every single small business that exists on this planet can be the most successful small business in the world if you go through each of the ten principles and apply them. You will see that each of them call you out of yourself to reach for something higher than you are, and in the process of doing that, something truly remarkable happens. It happens again and again and again—the ten principles never fail.

I'll say to anyone who is reading this, that's exactly what you need to do. Go read _The Most Successful Small Business in the World_ and acquaint yourself with the ten principles, and suddenly you'll be in a new world. That's why I say that anyone's business can become the most successful small business in the world, because the world we're speaking about is a completely different world than the world most of us live in.

I: What can we expect from you in the next year?

MG: We've started two new companies over the past fifteen months, the first of which is called Michael E. Gerber Partners. Michael E. Gerber Partners is really a social network—a business network—that effectively enables every vertical market in the world—whether that vertical market be a chiropractor or an optometrist or a financial advisor, etc.—to truly understand how to apply the E-Myth point of view. Go to work *on your company* not *in your company*. Create a company that works *without you* as opposed to *because of you*.

To apply that and to do that, I'm seeking out individuals to co-author these vertical E-Myth books. We have nine books that have already been published or are on their way to being published including *The E-Myth Chiropractor* and *The E-Myth Optometrist*. We've also recently published *The E-Myth Attorney: Why Most Legal Practices Don't Work and What to Do About It.*

There are 310 vertical markets that we're focusing our attention on over the next three years, which means there will be 310 new E-Myth books written through the eyes and voice of the generalist, that's me, and the specialists, which are my co-authors who have taken the E-Myth point of view and applied it in a profound way to truly transform the state of their practice so they can go out and teach their peers in their market and in their industry. They show other chiropractors, other optometrists, other financial advisors, etc. how to apply it as they have.

As we begin to do that, we see it as the largest social network of its kind in the world, raising all businesses in every industry to a level of performance and productivity unlike anything that's ever been done before. That's one company.

The second company is called Origination, and it's the new venture development process by which we engage the unemployed, the under-employed, the self-employed, and sole proprietors in a process that begins with The Dreaming Room and takes them through four distinct steps: Leap, Affirm, Launch, and Grow. We call this the New Venture Development Process, and through this program we expect to start hundreds of thousands of micro companies by engaging the entrepreneur within each and every one of those founders. Our aim is to teach people who normally depend upon a job—and who can no longer depend upon a job—that they don't *have* to depend on getting the job. In fact, we help them to realize they can create jobs for countless other individuals while teaching them at the same time how to awaken the entrepreneur within themselves. It's a revolutionary economic development program and process, the likes of which we've not seen before.

That's a window into what we'll be doing over the next year.

I: It's incredible. Would you mind if we move now into a few personal questions, starting with what inspires you?

MG: What inspires me is creating. I love to create. I cannot *not* create. Creating is key. Without creating, life is meaningless. I believe in earnest that if we're born in the image of God, and I believe we are, we're born to create. Here we are on this earth. We're born to fix the world, and there are an infinite number of things we could do. Those things are simply calling to us, and to the degree we're awake and looking, we will see them. They're so exciting and enticing when you begin to understand how broken the world is and yet how extraordinarily remarkable it is to fix it.

That's what I do. I continue in the pursuit of my dream, my vision, my purpose, and my mission, which hasn't changed in the past forty years. My dream is the same. My vision is the same. My purpose is the same. My mission is the same. I simply pursue it to discover how to do it better than it's ever been done, and that process is endless. I know I'll not figure it all out, but that's part of what's so exciting about it—I know someone will.

I: How do you inspire others and change their lives?

MG: Very simply. I write books and I speak. I just came back from an event in Las Vegas where I was a keynote speaker. The event started out with a discussion on growing a business. By the time I was done, people were crying. People were coming up to me and asking, "How do I get to feel that way?" I had to say to them, "You *are* feeling that way. You can't help but feel that way. It's why we're here."

As we begin to do that—to write books, to speak, and to create companies that have a profound impact on the people who work there, the people who buy from us, the people who are developers with us, and so forth—all of those things come together to have a profound impact.

I know there's going to be, as it's been said, a tipping point, meaning that point in one's life when true transformation of the small business occurs. We've awakened the entrepreneur within millions of people. We don't know what that tipping point will be or when it will be, but we know the fundamental principles are true because we've applied them again and again. We've watched these principles take effect in every kind of business possible and individual possible, and we've seen them have a truly transformational impact, so I know we're doing the right thing. All we have to do is to continue to pursue it with everything we've got, and in the process we will awaken the entrepreneur within millions upon millions of people in the world. As we do that, I honestly believe the world will be shifted onto a completely new plane.

I: What made you choose this arena for your life's great work?

MG: Who knows? First, I was doing this, then I was doing that, and now here I am. The truth is, if we look back to the day when I started my first company in 1977, no one at that time would have been able to say that I would be successful in this.

I didn't know anything about business. I'd been a hippie when there were hippies, a beatnik when there were beatniks, a jazz saxophone player, a framer of houses, and I wanted to become a contractor. I had absolutely no notion that I would be doing this at all until a friend of mine asked me to do him a favor. That favor led me to realize that I had been under the impression that everyone who owned a business knew what they were doing; I suddenly discovered they didn't, and I was called to it.

Who knows when these things are going to happen to you? You cannot possibly know when that epiphany is going to strike you and you're going to be called to something. All you can do is live your life as though it's about to come, and it will. When it does, it will be the most extraordinary moment when you suddenly awaken and see what you've been missing.

I: You probably get this question a lot, but what advice would you offer to someone who is thinking about starting a new business?

MG: Stop! Don't start that business. Come dream with me. Come to The Dreaming Room. At Origination, we are certifying Dreaming Room facilitators. I did The Dreaming Room fifty-eight times myself, all to the point where I would be able to invent a system so that I could turn around to someone like you and say, "Would you like to have this impact on people you know who are considering starting a business? Would you like to have this impact on people who are stuck and perhaps unemployed or simply don't know where to go or what to do? You can, because we can teach you how to do that."

"Creating a job for yourself is the worst thing you could possibly do. Create a dream, a vision, a purpose, and a mission for yourself."

Our intent is to have thousands upon thousands of Dreaming Room facilitators around the world. We now have facilitators in Colombia, Sweden, Denmark, and South Africa, and another who just left the training to go back to Sydney, Australia to start conducting Dreaming Rooms there. This is taking off throughout the world.

To anyone who thinks they're going to start a business, I would say please don't start your business yet. Before you ever write a business plan, before you ever open your door, come dream with me to discover your passion. Discover the meaning of the business you wish to create. You have to discover the profoundly important reason for doing this other than simply creating a job for yourself. Creating a job for yourself is the worst thing you could possibly do.

Create a dream, a vision, a purpose, and a mission for yourself. No business will fail that is absolutely consumed by those four words. Once that happens, you'll begin it in exactly the way that is necessary for you to build a scalable model so it can be replicated successfully again and again, just like the McDonald's hamburger stand was.

I: Michael, thank you for sharing so much of your passion with us. Walt Disney once said, "I can't believe there are any heights that can't be scaled by a man who knows the secret of making dreams come true." I consider you the Walt Disney for small businesses.

MG: No one has ever called me that before, but I love it!

Chapter
2

Happiness = Profit
Business Formula
Dr. Cathy Greenberg

Chapter 2
Happiness = Profit Business Formula
Dr. Cathy Greenberg

Dr. Cathy Greenberg, a *NY Times* best-selling author, helps executives and employees maximize their potential using her unique Happiness = Profit business formula. Having done so successfully for more than two decades, she wins rave reviews from clients as well as from leadership gurus including Warren Bennis, Marshall Goldsmith, and Noel Tichy.

I: First of all, what inspires you?

CG: A lot of things inspire me. What I guess would be of interest to readers is what inspired me to be interested in the science of happiness—why I spend so much time researching it, writing about it, and talking about it.

The real reason is because I've experienced it as a result of my own triumph over tragedy. I was a managing partner in a very well-known firm called Accenture and part of the Computer Sciences Corporation—two of the largest consulting firms in the world.

I was traveling on a daily basis to far and wonderful parts of the world, serving our client base and doing executive and strategic coaching, and I wound up with two potentially terminal illnesses. Basically, I hit the wall of life after going through a divorce, losing my parents, and experiencing the loss of a child while I was pregnant. I realized I had to get it together; even though I was considered successful by society's indications of success in terms of title, income, and lifestyle, I was not happy.

I took the time down here on earth to get it together, and I learned a lot about the science of happiness and positive psychology. Being a behavioral scientist, I was able to apply what I knew to myself, and then turned it into a model that I now use to help others as well.

I: That's fantastic. How do you touch others and change their lives?

CG: I feel that when people are truly ready to make a bold change, they will start to realize that happiness is not something you seek, but rather that it is found in the things you *do* in life such as offering and receiving forgiveness, growing friendships, and pursuing wisdom and knowledge in terms of learning and seeking information. When you deliver on your sense of purpose in a way that enables others to achieve their goals, then happiness follows. Happiness is not something we seek. It's not an ego-based approach to life. It is something we *do*. And in the process of doing it for others, we gain it ourselves.

"Happiness is not something we seek. It's not an ego-based approach to life. It is something we do. And in the process of doing it for others, we gain it ourselves."

I: How is happiness related to personal and professional profit?

CG: Well, it's fascinating to me that since I wrote *What Happy Companies Know* in 2005—which was the launch of our company, H2C, LLC—we have seen the release of programs by wonderful leaders like John Mackey at Whole Foods that are what we refer to as "consciousness of capitalism." Happiness has a lot to do with profit because when you are happy, you are joyful; when you are in a joyful state, you are in fact in a state of pleasure; when you are in a state of pleasure, you are fully engaged in whatever it is that you are doing; when you are fully engaged, your performance increases. Follow that line of thinking to the end of that stream of words: HAPPINESS = joy = pleasure = engagement = performance = PROFIT. Profit, therefore, is a natural predisposition that follows.

I: Is Happiness = Profit a psychological state, a behavior, or a true science?

CG: I consider happiness to be a true science and also a way of being. It is a conscious effort. Being happy is defined by many different people in many different cultures in many different ways. I've traveled around the world talking to people who study happiness—people who are well published like Martin Seligman,

Sonja Lyubomirsky, Barbara Fredrickson, and Kim Cameron. I could go on and on, but essentially happiness, when it's fully engaged, leads our lives on a path to do better things for others and for ourselves. As a result, we create a state of consciousness where happiness becomes an important component of what we do. So you might say that happiness is a behavior. To me, it is a behavior that enables health and wellness and ultimately profitability, both personally and professionally.

I: How can happiness make a difference in my life or my own self-improvement programs?

CG: I love that question. I love helping others begin to see the connection between happiness and profit in a simple formula.

When we're fully engaged in what we are doing and we're present, our performance increases significantly. Could you imagine if you could engage the full capacity of a person you're coaching? You can engage the heart and mind of an individual in so many ways, and the easiest way to start is by asking them a very simple question: "What inspires you?" or "What are you inspired by?" When you use the words *what are you* and the word *inspired* in whatever form you want, an engagement process begins, because using the words *you* and *inspiration* will automatically trigger an idea or a thought that engages another human being in something that's focused on them that's good, and that's where you begin.

The science of happiness is about looking at what's right, and from there you find the one small element, and—if I could refer to the example of a little grain of sand inside the shell of a pearl-producing oyster—you start to see the layers of happiness grow. From that little gritty piece of sand you then start to create layers of goodness. You do that by looking at what's right, and you create one pearl. Then, over time, you string the pearls and you see more goodness. It's very hard for someone who's coaching another person using this philosophy, this strength, and this language to create anything less than a bracelet or a necklace in a very short period of time. When you focus a person on what's right, they will build on it faster, quicker, and better, and it becomes an amazing opportunity to see people grow.

I: Is it worth my time to focus on happiness in today's economy?

CG: It would be foolish for anyone who is thinking about this tough economy *not* to focus on happiness. It's something we all owe ourselves. Happiness is an important component to health and wellness. In our new book, *What Happy Working Mothers Know,* which is the third book in the series, we refer to the acronym *HAPPY*. If you're coaching someone, it's a very simple model to use as a formula to begin.

Health: The *H* is such an exciting opportunity, especially when you look at the resolutions you've made for the year, and it stands for Health. What one thing can you do to improve your health that will make you better at what you do in everything else? Can you get more exercise? Spend more time outdoors? Eat better? Drink more water? Consume less sugar? It's one small step to build on.

Adaptation: The *A* stands for Adaptation. Can you adapt to your world by doing less while recognizing that sometimes less is more?

Proud (of Your Family): The first *P* stands for being Proud of your family. Recognize that no one is perfect and that everyone has problems. One in three people in this world are touched by cancer or alcoholism or some other type of illness.

Proud (of Your Work): The second *P* stands for being Proud of your work. Find something at work every day that you can be proud of. Don't focus on what didn't go well or on the 5 or 10% of your day that wasn't perfect; instead, look at the past week and consider the small things you did well. Ask yourself how your week could end on a high note even if it's been one of the worst weeks of your life.

Young: The *Y* stands for being Young at heart. Remember to laugh at yourself, laugh often, and find reasons to laugh. It's so easy to find reasons *not* to because the news provides us with so much negative information—bleeding leads. Look for opportunities to smile and for opportunities to catch others doing the same.

I: How did you become interested in this subject, and how did you become an expert on the science of happiness?

CG: I became interested in this back in early 2000. As I said, I was diagnosed with two potentially terminal illnesses. I was a high-producing executive in one of the world's largest consulting firms. I was high on life and extremely happy and capable. My world came crashing down when I hit that wall of life, learning that I had created my own illnesses through stress and travel, and that the people around me were disengaging from me because, while I loved them, I wasn't there enough for them to love me. I began by learning how human flourishing works.

Here I am almost a decade later having written three books on the subject, having spoken perhaps on every continent around the world, and having worked with clients from Sydney to Dubai. I have a lot to learn, but there are enough people who have been reading and learning along with me who would say that I'm certainly a thought leader in this area and have the client profile to prove it.

I: What research have you done or what have you written on the subject?

CG: Well, the three books, obviously. The newest one, which is a number one *Wall Street Journal* business book and a number two *New York Times* best seller is *What Happy Working Mothers Know,* which I co-authored with Barrett Avigdor. Thousands of women from around the world contributed to that book via online research conducted by wonderful companies that helped us to get the survey out there electronically, and Barrett Avigdor, my co-author, conducted face-to-face interviews with groups from around the world. We were just thrilled to have done that research.

The prior book, *What Happy Women Know,* co-authored with Dan Baker, was based on the stories of hundreds of women who have moved from tragedy to triumph. The book prior to that, *What Happy Companies Know,* is based on the global Fortune 500 and of course the ongoing Fortune 100 that we would all want to work for. I'm always researching, working with clients who are interested in the subject, and writing about it.

I: What inspires you to write?

CG: I believe life experiences are truly at the root of anyone's desire to write. In my case, my life experiences, while unique to me, have led to life discoveries that might be applicable to someone else's unique experience.

I've been very fortunate in my life, and I choke up a little bit when I say that. As a result, I find it important at this stage of my career to help and support others in their personal mission. I'm trying to pay it forward by helping as many people as I can in the time that I have. My passion for writing comes from that desire to help others.

I: How does your writing inspire others?

CG: While writing the past couple of books, I found a sense of connection with a variety of people, not only in the global community of serving businesses, but also with working families that serve businesses. I've been fortunate to talk to global leaders, business professionals, working moms who work inside the home, and working moms who work outside the home, and I have learned a great deal about their experiences, which I've been able to capture and share with others.

"I've been fortunate in my life. As a result, I find it important at this stage of my career to support others in their personal mission. I'm trying to pay it forward by helping as many people as I can."

Whether you're working with a mom, supervising or managing a mom, or you're a mom who is managing and supervising others including the people in your household, all of the things that I have learned over the years and the nine books that I have contributed to seem to have come through with meaning. That makes me very happy.

I: How would you define success as it pertains to writing?

CG: For me, it's getting a very salient point across using as few words as possible. I do that in writing much better than I do it in speaking. There is a definite difference when it comes to the number of words men and women use, and I use far too many.

I: What is your most powerful writing moment?

CG: My most powerful writing moment to date has been a testimonial to my mother who has passed. She was a wonderful woman who inspired me to be independent and to celebrate my experiences in life. My mother was not a highly educated woman in the classic sense; she barely graduated from high school. She was a burlesque dancer, and she was a fascinating human being who studied people quite well. I think I get my emotional intelligence and my street smarts from my mother.

I wrote a preface and testimonial to my mother for the book I wrote with Dr. Dan Baker, *What Happy Women Know*. Unfortunately, the editor chose to ignore that testimonial to my mother and thought it did not fit the tone of the book.

That's an example of how being inspired can sometimes be thwarted by the people who make decisions about what makes a book successful. What I thought would make the book engaging and what the editors, the publisher, and our professional writers thought would make it engaging were very different. I learned a great lesson from that experience.

I: What are the three most important personal tips you can share for achievement and fulfillment through writing?

CG: That's a great question, because I think it's going to be very different for everyone. I'm sure that people have expectations that often are not met; I just gave you a great example of this. But there are three keys for helping to align those expectations. There are three things that cause a relationship to fall into what we call a "breakdown." The same kinds of things can happen to you as a writer if you're not clear on what those expectations are.

Aligning Your Writing Expectations

What is your vision? Are you writing because it's going to make you happy, or are you writing because there are lessons you can share that others can use, apply, and follow much more expeditiously by having it all in one place and because you think it has a general application?

A lot of people ask me about writing a book, and they go into a beautiful dissertation on why everyone should read this book about them. We love to be our own best subject, and anyone who's a professional interviewer knows that if you ask someone a good, curious question about themselves, you'll have a great interview. The problem is that we don't often think about the application of our subject—us—in comparison to the general population.

You have to be smart about how you choose to tell your story; the vision for your book is so important. Are you writing it for yourself or for someone else? I often tell someone who is writing a book for themselves, "Write that book and self-publish it, put it on Facebook, or put it anywhere you like for people to access it. See what kind of response you get before you go through the process of creating a book outline, submitting it to an agent, and preparing to challenge the publishing community to publish it."

Who is your audience? Who do you want to read this book? This is very important and is closely related to your expectations. A book should appeal to all of the different Myers-Briggs types. You wouldn't think about that under normal circumstances. You would think that if someone likes the title, they're going to pick up the book, look through the introduction and the index, and consider your message. But not everyone reads a book that way.

You have to write a book for all of the Myers-Briggs types, because some people are going to want to follow the book from A to B, B to C, and C to D. Other people are going to read chapter one and chapter four and chapter nine. Some people want to see a detailed index so they can see if their favorite author or some information that perhaps they have been working on is included in the book. Some people are great social networkers and they want to see what kinds of stories you have—are they engaging? Then there are people who love tools and job aides, and they want to go through the book and locate the self-help or teachable point of view, as Noel Tichy would say.

When you come to understand that Myers-Briggs inventory, you can clearly write a book for all; you can allow it to be *your* book while also enabling it to flow for the purpose of the reader.

Is the book easy to read and accessible? Is the book pithy, on-point, and subject appropriate? For example, I wrote *Global Leadership: The Next Generation* with Marshall Goldsmith in our groundbreaking research, which he still writes about in *What Got You Here Won't Get There* and *Mojo,* and that seminal piece was based on a global study we did together.

Through that process, I learned how to apply data. If you're going to be pithy and seminal, you have to take into consideration who's reading it, how much time they have, how long a chapter is, and how a chapter can be helpful to someone in a short period of time. It was the same issue with *What Happy Working Mothers Know.*

You've got someone's attention for a period of time. Do you write your book like a good novel, making the reader want to read the next chapter, or do you write it as a stand-alone piece, so that within fifteen minutes, a busy individual can pick it up, find what they need, and move on, not necessarily having to read it in the order in which it is written?

I have had the privilege of working with a great group of people who specialize in these kinds of psychological analyses behind writing a book. I can truly say that one of the reasons why *What Happy Working Mothers Know* is a number two *New York Times* best-selling book and a number one *Wall Street Journal* book is because we followed those principles, and I will do that with every book I create going forward.

I: Tell me how these three things work for you.

CG: As far as having a vision, I'm a team writer. I like having great minds producing content that's excellent, rich, and diverse. When you have co-authors, as I did with all of my books, you want to make sure you share a common vision and a common goal.

There is a set of principles that you operate within because, in most instances—as we know from *Global Leadership: The Next Generation* by Marshall Goldsmith and my friend Alastair Robertson, a former partner of mine from Accenture, and Maya Hu-Chan, a specialist in multicultural global leadership—you have to know where everyone's sweet spot is or, as our friend Marcus Buckingham would say, where those strengths lie.

Using a great set of instruments—for example, my friends at Talent Plus have a wonderful instrument for determining where your strengths lie—you can parse up a team's responsibilities and roles so that everyone is doing what they love to do, which is self-motivating, and you broaden and build on those strengths.

Practicing our strengths makes us better at what we do. Continuing to use those three points and making sure we're all aligned is very important.

It's not just about a book outline, a publisher that loves the idea, and a PR team that's going to get behind the book, it's the team that creates that energy. Those three points—vision, audience, and adaptability—are key to making sure a team works well together.

I: What are your favorite writing tools?

CG: I don't think I have any favorite tools; what I do have is a perspective on situations that I'm privileged to be a part of.
For example, I am in the process of creating a program right now for the United States Navy, and I feel very privileged and honored to be

asked to be a speaker at our special forces training center. I'm going to talk to those who are on active duty, and then I'm going to speak to their families. I look forward to hearing their stories and to being in the moment when I capture perhaps just a statement that is somehow reflective of something that is going to pull—in my mind and in my heart—the spirit of a story. It will be a story that will be crafted based on many stories, so that a compendium of situations become a subject that can be built upon, and then a lesson learned. Hopefully, others will feel as strongly about those subjects as I do.

We have to protect people's names—obviously these are people who need to be protected for a lot of reasons—and we also need to express their story in an honest and authentic way.

What makes me want to write is listening to people's stories, finding a way to put them together in a meaningful way, delivering them to the audience, and making them say, "Ah ha!" That makes a lot of sense to me. And having heard the stories in this way, I can then take them apart, learn from them, and create a tool that I can put at the end of each story to help someone see and reflect on their own situation.

"What makes me want to write is listening to people's stories, finding a way to put them together in a meaningful way, delivering them to the audience, and making them say, 'Ah ha!'"

I: What books have influenced your life most?

CG: The Warren Bennis books have been extremely influential on me. Warren has been one of my mentors, Marshall has been a dear friend and research partner, and Noel Tichy has been a dear friend and advisor. I've also worked with wonderful people like Edgar Schein, who I recently saw again at the Linkage OD Summit in Chicago. I am very blessed to work with so many incredible people. I have been blessed to have received advice and support through our radio show from people like Sonja Lyubomirsky and Jim Kouzes.

The reason I mention the names of these people is because they've all written salient books. They've all written on the subject that I have now started to build upon, and that is leadership, the science of happiness, and emotional intelligence. Obviously that list of names would also include Daniel Goleman, Marty Seligman, and others. They have all written practical books. The books that have touched me in terms of storytelling include *Jane Eyre* and *Frankenstein*—classics that tell a story within a story. A lot of what I try to do in my business books is to write stories within stories.

I: What advice do you have for other writers?

CG: Do what makes you proud and happy that you've decided to put your work out there in whatever format you've chosen. Whatever you want to do, do it.

I continually hear people say, "I want to write a book—I have a book in me." Everyone has their own bucket list. I will be honest with you, my bucket list never had "write a book" on it. That was never on my bucket list—not in my wildest dreams. My bucket list is simple, and fortunately, my life has been extraordinary, so all of the things that people typically put on their bucket list—jumping out of a plane, writing a book, or seeing the world—have already been checked off for me.

Right now I am focused on living a happy, full, and healthy life with a partner who loves and respects me. I want to watch my children have their own children, to look at the world through their eyes, and to understand these generational and exponentially different human beings we're creating all the time.

I have worked with actors and actresses who are trying to write poetry or their life story, sports celebrities who are trying to write a story that helps to put kids on the right path, and women who want to write their story simply because it's a healing process. Recently, I have supported former Miss Virginia and Teen Success Coach for MTV's MADE, Julie Marie Carrier, in creating her book, *BeYOUtiful,* which is touching the lives of young women and helping to build their confidence. It's such a joy to listen to what people want to write about and then help them find a way to distribute it that has meaning for them.

So, if you want to write, write. It doesn't matter whether anyone reads it. What matters is that you wrote it, and it has served a purpose—it touches the hearts, spirits, minds, and souls of many people.

It will eventually get to where it needs to go, which is a testimonial to books we now know very well like the *Harry Potter* series or the *Chicken Soup for the Soul* series. I could go on mentioning books that have been self-published and eventually wound up where they needed to be because someone saw the value in the story. That's the secret—when someone else sees the value in your story.

I: Tell us your latest news.

CG: I have a new book series in the works titled *Fearless*, hopefully for release in 2012-2013. The first book co-authored with TC North, *Fearless Leaders*, is a new genre in the happiness series. *Fearless* is all about demonstrating your highest level of appreciation for your strengths, talents, and experiences. It will be packed with usable insights, engaging stories, tools, and techniques to show you how to be truly *Fearless* in everything you choose to do. Stay tuned at www.TheFearlessBookSeries.com. (Coming in December 2012.)

I also have a new venture with my partner, Dr. Relly Nadler, who is an author himself. We have a Web site called XCEL Institute, which stands for eXcellence in Coaching for Executive Leadership at www.xcelinstitute.com. From there, you can find Relly Nadler's Web site and my Web site where all of our books are found.

Finally, I would like to add that this book is a wonderful mechanism for helping people understand where their true gifts might lie by giving people the motivation and the coaching and the sensitive viewpoint of the people you have interviewed. You are providing a genuine and helpful resource. There are so many people out there who are chomping at the bit to get their message out for so many reasons; establishing what that reason is and who might be the right audience for them is so helpful. I know that that's where you are going to be the most successful in helping people.

Happiness Tip From Cathy: Start every day by having one small thought: What are you going to do that's going to make a difference for you and others? What is it you're going to pursue? At the end of that day, take inventory, and look at one bright, small thing you did that made a difference. It may have only touched one person for one moment, but it made a difference, and those are the small things in life that build up. They become the pearls. At the end of the week, you'll have enough pearls to string a bracelet. At the end of a month, you'll have enough pearls to string a necklace.

Chapter
3

Emotional Intelligence, Performance, and Prosperity
Dr. Relly Nadler

Chapter 3
Emotional Intelligence, Performance, and Prosperity
Dr. Relly Nadler

Dr. Relly Nadler was educated as a clinical psychologist and is a world-class executive coach, corporate trainer, and author. He is the President and CEO of True North Leadership, Inc., an executive and organizational development firm, as well as the co-founder of the XCEL Institute, which stands for eXcellence in Coaching for Executive Leadership.

Dr. Nadler brings his expertise in emotional intelligence to his keynotes, consulting, coaching, and training. He has designed and delivered many multi-day executive boot camps for high achievers and for Fortune 500 companies.

Currently Dr. Nadler's work involves developing, identifying, and teaching tools for organizations, teams, and individuals to increase emotional intelligence and become star performers. As a co-host of Leadership Development News, a weekly online radio show on Voice America, he interviews leaders, authors, and consultants about their secrets.

I: What are the main leadership errors you see when it comes to the organizations and executives you work with?

RN: As an executive coach who has been inside a lot of organizations, I have witnessed six key leadership errors.

Six Key Leadership Errors

1. Generalization of Skill: When leaders have a technical skill in one area, we often assume that it will generalize into leadership.

They may be good at managing themselves as an individual performer and they rise up in the ranks. There is the sense that if they're good in a particular area, they will also make a good leader.

2. Spotlight Error: The president of a company I work with said that as a leader, you are in a glass box. All the good you do in a year can—in one selfish, undisciplined moment—be undone, and you lose all the emotional equity you've built up. We see this happen all the time in the media.

3. Influence Error: Often leaders they don't realize how much influence they have over others, and as a consequence, I think they often underperform as does their team. This is due in part to the spotlight error but also because emotions are contagious. The leader is the emotional thermostat for the team, meaning that their emotions are the most contagious for anyone on the team. If the leader is hot, irritated, and stressed out, their team is likely to be hot, irritated, and stressed out. If the leader is calm, cool, and deliberate, their team is likely to mirror that.

4. Neglect Error: All of this great leadership stuff that we do can easily get neglected or relegated in favor of the crisis or the hot issue of the day. The leadership functions of inspiring, giving direction, providing feedback, and delegating can easily be put off. The leader says, "Oh, I'll do that when I get a chance." Well, they don't always get that chance.

5. Alignment Error: The leader does not always align their style with the style of the people they are leading. The leader may give one person a lot of details, but if they do that with someone else, that person may feel over-managed. The leader needs to be flexible and change their style. Assessments can be helpful with this.

6. Focus Error: Followers want and expect their leaders to be well intentioned, to have thought-out plans, to be clear in their direction, and to know how a follower can contribute to the vision and what each follower's strengths are. Leaders may not have enough time to think about all of this, but followers hang on their words and expect this kind of focus and direction. The leader needs to take a little more time up front and consider what they're really saying and what they really want to see happen.

I: What are the characteristics of top performers, and why are they important for corporations and coaches to understand in terms of correcting these six leadership errors?

RN: These leadership errors are very common, and a lot of the characteristics of the top 10% of performers include emotional intelligence competencies.

How smart someone is and their level of technical expertise is often directly related to the level at which they enter into the work world. As someone moves up, it's in relation to the world of emotional intelligence, which is about understanding and managing one's self and others. The more they can do those things, the more that will move them into the top 10% of performers as they advance in an organization. A lot of this has to do with relationships. A lot of it has to do with knowing yourself. The number one reason a person leaves their job is because they don't feel appreciated. That usually comes from their relationship and interactions with their boss, so this contributes to the retention factor.

Some research has shown that 50% of life satisfaction comes from a person's relationship with his or her boss. When I first heard that, I thought it sounded pretty high. But your boss is inside your head, and if you have a bad boss—or even a good boss who's emotional intelligence skills may be low—that probably does affect your life satisfaction at a rate of as much as 50%.

I: I agree. You typically spend eight hours each day working around your boss, so that's a lot of time. When you go home, you're still thinking and ruminating about what happened.

RN: Yes, and you can't just get rid of that. If someone is saying, "I can't believe they didn't see this," or "I don't know why they said that," or "I can't understand why this is going on," that's taking up brain time; they're not being creative, they're not being innovative, and they're not thinking about new ways to deal with either a product or the people they are involved with.

I: How would you define emotional intelligence?

RN: It is basically about understanding yourself. There's a personal side and a social side. The personal side includes things like confidence, accurate self-assessment, how you mange yourself, initiative, trustworthiness, and achievement orientation.

The social side involves understanding and managing others, or relationship management. This side includes things like empathy, service orientation, how you get ahead in an organization, political savvyness, leadership, influence, initiating change, and developing others. Those are some of the key areas in each of these clusters of emotional intelligence.

I: Why is training in emotional intelligence so important?

RN: It is important to learn about your emotions and what's happening in regards to social pain. How would you handle someone who is ruminating about that? As coaches, we are able to talk about these things with someone. We now know that just talking about emotions is called affect labeling and allows the person to regain more cognitive control.

Part of emotional intelligence is about understanding so that you can manage your own emotions. Just talking with a coach can help you to be less reactive and less emotional.

The good news is that you can learn these emotional intelligence skills whereas your IQ is basically static. How do you manage yourself? How do you have a tough conversation with someone who is a direct report? How do you avoid beating around the bush? What do you do to differentiate your leadership style when it comes to Generation Y versus the Millennials? How do you lead a change initiative? These are all things you can learn through emotional intelligence training and specifically in terms of these competencies.

Tips for Raising Emotional Intelligence for New Leaders
- **Be clear** about what your top five responsibilities are.
- **Be clear with your team** about what you want to see happen.
- **Learn about individual and team strengths**—talk to them.
- **Communicate with your team** regarding the best ways to work with you.
- **Be aware if you are adding too much value.** New leaders may try to add too much value and take away the team commitment to carry out.
- **Have one-on-one meetings with your people** and talk about some of these things.
- **Self manage—be aware of what your triggers are.** If you are not aware of them, the 360 feedback can help. Talk with your team, with friends, or with a spouse. It is important identify triggers so they don't become derailers.

Chapter
4

Fulfill Your Purpose Through a Thriving Business
Kendall SummerHawk

Chapter 4

Fulfill Your Purpose Through a Thriving Business

Kendall SummerHawk

Kendall SummerHawk believes that you deserve to be financially successful by fulfilling your soul's divine purpose via a thriving business, and that making great money is an important part of your spiritual path.

She is the author of the book *Brilliance Unbridled* and many best-selling home study programs such as *How to Charge What You're Worth and Get It!*, *Seven Money Mindset & Pricing Strategy Secrets of an Authentic Million Dollar Marketing Coach*, and *How to Add Six Figures to Your Business Practically Overnight With Lucrative, High-End, Platinum Style Coaching Programs*. Kendall's business is the perfect model for creating a seven-figure business.

I: What keeps entrepreneurs from charging what they're worth?

KS: This is a great question. There are three factors I see that keep entrepreneurs from charging what they're worth.

Three Factors That Keep Entrepreneurs From Charging What They're Worth

1. Comparing Themselves to Others: Most of the time when entrepreneurs compare themselves to others, guess who ends up with the short end of the stick? They don't compare themselves and say, "Okay, great, I'm more experienced or better than they are, and I should charge more." They usually compare themselves and say, "Oh gosh, I don't have that level of experience. I don't have that level of credibility." They tear themselves down and end up suppressing their fees.

2. Not Understanding the True Value of What They Do: They look at the mechanical pieces of what they do, such as how much time they spend with someone, the features they offer, and the logistical pieces. Then they say, "Well, that can't be worth that much." What they really want to be looking at, of course, is the value of the transformation they're creating for their clients. It's not about how much time you spend with someone, it's about the transformation that occurs for them.

3. Discounting Themselves: This is true particularly for female entrepreneurs. They discount what they do naturally and easily. They say, "Oh, that's so easy for me, that can't be worth very much." Or they'll say, "Gosh, I haven't been doing this very long, it can't be worth much." They discount themselves in a variety of ways, and that shows up in their fees as discounting their pricing. Discounting themselves leads to discounting their pricing.

I: Women discount themselves even in the corporate environment outside of coaching when they go into their assessments. They belittle their own skills, which is interesting because men typically don't do that. Men say, "I'm worth it."

KS: That's very true. Of course, when we're working for ourselves, these things show up in our fees. If someone is working at a job, it may result in them not getting a promotion or the salary they deserve. But the end result is consistently fee related.

I: Why do so many entrepreneurs think that making money goes against being spiritually authentic?

KS: People in general think this, and of course it carries over into the entrepreneurial world. Somewhere over the course of time—and I'm sure it has been going on for hundreds if not thousands of years—that idea has become a stronger and stronger imprint. We began by automatically believing a rich person must be greedy. My story used to be that rich people were thoughtless and insensitive. At least that's what I would tell myself, and I could look around and find plenty of evidence for that. Of course, there's also plenty of evidence that rich people are thoughtful, generous, caring, and sensitive too, but those were not the examples I was willing to see. Those examples didn't pass through my filter—my judgment.

The media also plays into this mind-set through television, movies, books, articles, etc. As a culture, we idolize those who are "spiritual" and are "good people" even though they are poor—those who are giving so much of themselves that they have nothing left.

We don't show examples of men and women who are successful, wealthy people as well as generous, good people doing great work. Part of this may be due to the fact that people who are very wealthy and who are doing great work don't go around bragging about it. They just do their thing. They're quite philanthropic. They lead a lot of causes but they don't make a big deal about it. So we may not be hearing about them quite as much.

> *"Making money is part of your spiritual path. When you are fully on your spiritual path, you are being a good person. You are being creative. You are offering services or products that are of value and for the greater good of the world. You're making a positive difference for people."*

It's easy to pinpoint a villain, and it is even easier to choose someone who is making a lot of money to be that villain. If we start idolizing people who are successful financially *and* spiritually, well, we're going to have to pick a new villain.

The thing to keep in mind is that entrepreneurs look at it as either-or. They can have one or the other, but they can't have both, and that causes a conflict within. So they choose to be a good, spiritual person and not have any money, or they get into a really unhappy, uncomfortable, and unproductive conflict—a negotiation with themselves—and they make some money but then stop themselves at a certain dollar amount.

There's a formula I share for how to tell where that dollar amount is for each of us. What I believe—and what I see to be true in my life and in the lives of many of my clients—is that making money is part of your spiritual path. When you are fully on your spiritual path, you *are* being a good person. You are being creative. You are offering services or products that are of value and for the greater good of the world. You're making a positive difference for people.

Let me contrast that with someone who is helping only a few people. Let's say they are coaching ten or fifteen clients, which can sound like a lot, but it's actually not. They're operating on a very small scale. So yes, they're doing good work, but their realm of influence is so small that they are not really making the impact that they are capable of making, and they're not making very much money.

When someone is really stepping into their power and coming forward in a bold, beautiful, passionate, and well-organized way so that their business is helping them to create the maximum level of impact for the greatest number of people possible, they're going to make money. There's no way an entrepreneur can be rocking their spiritual path—helping as many people as they are supposed to in as big a way as they're supposed to—and not be making money.

That's why I say making great money is part of your spiritual path. There is an incredible transformation that needs to take place in someone's mind-set, heart, and energy in order for them to create a lot of income doing what they love. It pushes buttons for people and causes them to create some important breakthroughs, and those breakthroughs can happen in an instant.

When an entrepreneur is making those kinds of breakthroughs, coming into who they are supposed to be, and fulfilling their soul's divine purpose, there's no way they can't make great money at the same time; the two go hand in hand.

I: I can see how not having that mind-set would hinder you, because you would get in your own way and sabotage your efforts.

KS: Absolutely. I have the enviable position of having coached thousands of hours and thousands of people, and I see the same patterns over and over again. Of course, I've also seen the breakthroughs occurring over and over again, and that's a beautiful gift. I had to go through those breakthroughs myself, and I do have a seven-figure business. This year we expect to be in the multi-seven figures, which is really extraordinary.

I am so much more in my truth today than I have ever been. I know what it's like to have to make those breakthroughs, and that's why I can say with full confidence that they're actually really easy to make. It's actually easier to make a lot more money than it is to make less; it truly is.

There are two reasons behind why it is easier to make more than it is to make less. One reason is practical and one is energetic. On the practical side, it's easier to make more than less because to make more money, your business is going to need to have a lot of leverage in its design. We have hundreds of clients, and I say "we" because my husband, Richard, works with me in my business. Actually, almost every member of my family works with me in my business. It's really cool.

Richard is a trained coach, and so we co-lead programs together; some I lead and some he leads—it's really fabulous. We have hundreds of clients and a variety of different programs and they all involve coaching. These are not light, fluffy programs. These are programs that offer a lot of content and information in coaching because we really believe in coaching.

With all this leverage through the business design—and I coach people on how to create a business model that offers all this leverage—I work far less than I've ever worked. I don't even work full-time hours, and I make great money. That's why it's easier on a practical basis once you create leverage, and I can show someone who has five clients or two clients or no clients how to create that leverage immediately. It's very simple.

On the energetic side for why it is easier to make more than to make less, every time you experience a breakthrough, you step into a new level of creating income for yourself. This happens because you are shedding the old—letting go of old beliefs that have often been handed down through generations, old behaviors, and old ways of thinking that have been holding you back—and becoming more aligned and integrated with your truth and what you believe. These new beliefs empower you and initiate practical actions that help you create and maintain greater levels of income by doing what you love. Any time you are doing something that's so aligned, it's really simple.

I: You have a unique way of looking at pricing challenges. Would you share your views on undercharging, discounting, and overcharging?

KS: One of the models I've created was actually a divine download. I literally turn my eyes upward and thank God for channeling this through me because that's where it came from—total Source energy. What it is in a nutshell is that money situations, either positive or negative, always mirror where we stand with one of four things: boundaries, courage, our sense of deservability, and love.
Each of these four areas has very specific behaviors or indicators that show up in how a person handles their fees and even other

situations within their business. For example, an issue with boundaries will show up when it comes to discounts and over-delivering. Someone may charge a decent amount, but they consistently over-deliver. Or, often they make themselves too available and include everything but the kitchen sink in their packages. That tells me that there is an issue with deservability. There are similar symptoms evident when it comes to issues with courage and love.

Each area shows up in discounting, undercharging, not raising fees, or making money and not keeping it—I see that quite a bit. People follow that up-and-down rollercoaster: they make it, they don't have it, they make it, they don't have it.

That's the money mirror of love. There's a lot more information that goes into this model, but in a nutshell, that's one model I've created for how money relates to charging what you're worth and getting it.

I: What is the first thing an entrepreneur should do if he or she wants to start charging more?

KS: Let me begin by addressing the mind-set or energy that is associated with this issue, and then I'll address the practical side. The first thing to understand is that your current fees represent past thinking. They represent your past mind-set and beliefs about what you thought was possible. So, if you want your future income to be different—I'm assuming you want to make more money—you have to change your mind-set right now.

A practical step to take is to train yourself to get into the habit of focusing on the value of what you do for your clients. Consider the value of the result—the value of the transformation—that each client receives by choosing to hire you. It's not about how much time you invest, it's about the value of the transformation they experience.

As you can imagine, when an entrepreneur becomes clear on the value of the results their clients are experiencing—not just that a client has more clarity or feels better, those are vague results, but the specific results—no matter what kind of entrepreneur they are, they will look at what they have been charging and say, "Excuse me? No way! That's way too low!" It gives them a lot of confidence, and truthfully, how much someone ends up charging as a fee level has a little to do with who the client is and a lot to do with their own personal level of confidence.

I: What do you say to people who fear that if they raise their rates they will lose clients?

KS: I say sure, they might lose clients. I'm not going to guarantee that they won't lose clients. But it's okay.

Why it's Okay to Lose Clients When You Raise Your Fees

They are not the right fit. If you lose a client because you have raised your fees—whether it's an existing client or a prospective client—that person wasn't the right fit for you.

The increase will surpass the loss. Don't be afraid of losing income from loss of clients because the income you create from those new, higher fees is going to far surpass that lost income, even with fewer clients.

It doesn't happen as often as you might think. It really doesn't. So keep in mind—even if you lose a client or two—that it's really not that big a deal, because the clients you do get are actually going to be much more in alignment with the value that you are providing and they are receiving.

Clients who are aligned with that value, who really get it and say, "I want those results, and your fee is not a problem," make fantastic clients. They do the work, they show up, and they're engaged and involved. They get the results they were looking for, and you get great testimonials and referrals which help support higher fees. Everyone wins. So look at this as an opportunity to realign who you work with based on your new fees, and attract even better clients.

I: What is the biggest mistake entrepreneurs make regarding fees?

KS: The biggest mistake entrepreneurs make when it comes to pricing—besides comparing fees to others which is a huge mistake— is deciding what their clients can or cannot afford. I hear this all the time. People say, "No one is going to pay that. They're not going to be able to afford that."

I say, "Excuse me, you do not have the right to decide that for someone else." I get on a soapbox about this. As entrepreneurs, we do not have the right to decide for our clients what they can or cannot afford. It's none of our business. What *is* our business is to make sure that we are very clear about the value of the results our clients receive and that we communicate that value in a powerful, authentic, and specific way. Then it's up to each client to decide. There are plenty of people who will find the money to hire you.

I: How does undercharging hurt an entrepreneur's credibility?

KS: When you undercharge, you're not seen as credible; you're not viewed as an expert or as having any real value. We all mentally discount something that is

"The biggest mistake entrepreneurs make when it comes to pricing is deciding what their clients can or cannot afford. As entrepreneurs, we do not have the right to decide for our clients . . . It's none of our business."

inexpensive. In the same way, you're not taken seriously or viewed as someone who is going to be able to deliver something of value or of high quality, so that's how it hurts your credibility.

Let me offer some closing pieces of wisdom. First, raise your fees. It's very simple. This is not rocket science. And second, from a mind -set standpoint, keep in mind that when you increase your fees, you're going to change your life. Having more money is a beautiful thing. There is so much good you can do in the world when you have more money. It's really beautiful. Know that when you change your fees, you are changing your life. When you change your life, you are changing the lives of others. That's what I want people to remember.

Chapter
5

Grow Your Business With
Free Sessions That Sell!
Christian Mickelsen

Chapter 5
Grow Your Business With Free Sessions That Sell!
Christian Mickelsen

Christian Mickelsen is the author of *How to Quickly Get Started in Professional Coaching: The Truth About What it Really Takes.* He has been coaching for over ten years and has been seen in *Forbes, The Boston Globe,* Yahoo Finance, and MSN. He served for two years on the Board of Directors for the International Association of Coaching (IAC) and has created numerous support groups and products to help coaches become financially successful.

I: How did you get into coaching?

CM: I got into coaching as a client about twelve years ago. I first heard about the concept of coaching from Tony Robbins, and I started looking for a coach because my life was a total mess. I had started a business that was basically a money pit while I was still working at a job that I hated. I was out of shape and in a relationship that was not working. I didn't know what to do or how to get out of the mess I had gotten myself into, so I started looking for a coach and I found one. Nine months later my life had completely turned around. I was out of the job I hated, I was working for myself full time, I was back in great shape, and I was out of that relationship.

I discovered the power of coaching by becoming a client. Even though I had my own business and it was great that I was able to work for myself full time, it wasn't something I was passionate about; it was just an interesting business idea. I was really passionate about personal growth, and I thought maybe I could become a coach. I had a lot of self-doubts and limiting beliefs about who would want to listen to me. At the time, I assumed everyone in the world would want to be a coach, which I realize now is not true.

A lot of people aren't interested in that kind of stuff. Some people are very data-oriented—such as engineers—or they just prefer to do other things.

If you think everyone would want to do the thing that you want to do, that's a good clue that it's probably something you have strengths and interests in. You might think everyone would want to be a rock star. I don't know if I would really want to practice and play an instrument all the time. Clearly, playing a musical instrument is not something I'm passionate about. You might think everyone would want to be a movie star, but are you really passionate about acting and do you go to acting classes? Are you driven toward that kind of stuff? If you are, then that is probably a good fit for you, but it's not something that everyone wants to do, even though those are two careers—being a rock star and acting— that we think everyone would want to do.

Being a coach was one of those things for me. I felt like it would be so much fun and that I would love to be able to help people. I've always been someone that other people turn to for advice and for help. It's been that way pretty much my whole life, and I really care about people. But then I thought, *Who am I to do this? What would make me special? Would anyone even hire me?* I had to work through my own self-doubts, limiting beliefs, and fears about becoming a coach. The first client I ever had I coached for free; I felt like I would be happy if I didn't have to make money to pay bills so that I could continue to coach people for free. I just loved it.

Once I decided to go for it and to become a coach, I actually got six clients in my first month, and I just fell in love with it. I let my other business kind of wither on the vine. I still took care of some customers and handled some things that were happening, but I slowly let that business go as I ramped up my coaching business.

I found myself $72,000 in debt from the other business, and even though I got six clients in my first month, I was not charging the same coaching fees I do today. Today I am paid $9,500 per month per client, which is over $100,000 per year for each client. Back then I was only getting paid $195 per month per client, so even though I had six clients, I was making $1,200 a month. Unfortunately, that amount was definitely not enough to pay my mortgage and all of my other bills, especially with the debt I had incurred from my other business.

I struggled those first few years as a coach, but I was so happy and passionate about doing it. I fell behind on my mortgage every couple of months. It was a cycle: I'd get some clients and things would be going great, but then some clients would fall off and I'd be struggling again. It was really tough for those first few years, but those were good years too because I was fighting for something that really mattered—to be able to make a living doing something I loved that also made a difference in the world. It was a good challenge and I'm glad I stuck with it.

I finally got to the point where I was getting burned out, and I felt like I should either go back and get a job or just quit having to pay for things. I thought about continuing to coach but giving up my house. I thought that if I got rid of my house, my car, and everything I had to pay for, and became homeless, then I could coach people for free. I thought perhaps I could pay my way in society by coaching people. I thought maybe clients would take me into their house and give me a room to sleep in and a shower, that I could coach them and help them make some breakthroughs, and then I could move on to someone else's house.

I was so burned out from trying so hard to get clients. Some of my strategies were working and some weren't, but I didn't give up, I didn't get a job, and I didn't have to become homeless. I drew a line in the sand and I became even more committed to making it work. I read thirty-six books in thirty-six weeks and did everything I could to make my business work through trial and error. I tested many different things, I refined processes, and I got a system down that worked for getting clients.

Eventually I made my business quite successful, and then a small handful of coaches hired me to help them with their coaching businesses. Even though it took many years before I was making over $100,000 per year coaching, I was able to help four of the five coaches that hired me grow their businesses to over $100,000 a year within eighteen months, and some of them even faster. One coach went from zero to six figures within ninety days.

That's when I realized I could share all these things that I had to learn the hard way and that sharing those lessons could provide a huge shortcut for other coaches. They could get clients and grow their business a lot faster than I did. It was about five years ago when I decided to focus specifically on helping people get started in coaching, to get clients, and to grow to six-figure incomes.

I: You experienced the very transformation we aim for in coaching, and then learned from that to share it with others. It's amazing. You actually had a client go from zero to $100,000 in ninety days?

CM: I've actually helped coaches get really close to that in even shorter periods of time. Six figures annually would be $8,500 a month. The coach that went from zero to six figures in ninety days actually had six clients paying $1,500 a month within that time.

Another client I worked with about two years ago got five clients paying $1,300 a month within two weeks of our working together. That's just under a six-figure income right there. I kept telling him, "Just get one more client so you can be my fastest success story and go from zero to six figures in a month!" But he didn't want to have a lot of clients so I couldn't convince him to do it.

It's amazing how fast it can happen. People think that it takes years—and it *can* take years—but it doesn't have to take that long to get clients. There are so many little secrets, and if you do all these little things differently, they add up to fast results.

"If you're struggling with mental blocks, you could have all the best strategies and fastest shortcuts in the world, and there's still a good chance you're not going to be successful."

I: What is your secret for breaking through self-doubt and fear?

CM: I experienced a lot of self-doubt, fear, and limiting beliefs. Certainly learning more about marketing was very valuable and very helpful. Like I said, I read thirty-six books in thirty-six weeks. A lot of those books were business and marketing books, but a lot of them were also about personal growth and spiritual development.

I've heard people say that it's 80% mental and 20% technical or strategic. I don't know if those statistics are completely accurate, but I'll tell you what, if you're struggling with mental blocks, you could have all the best strategies and fastest shortcuts in the world, and there's still a good chance you're not going to be successful. On the other hand, if you have no mental blocks or even very few, then for you the 80% is going to be the how-to. Just learn how to do it, and once you know how, you can take off.

In the early days, I was so riddled with self-doubt, fear, limiting beliefs, and limiting thinking that my confidence went up and down like a roller coaster. Sometimes I'd feel super confident. I'd have some sessions with clients that would rock their world and they'd be really grateful. I'd get a couple new clients and I'd feel like the king of the world. Then I'd have some clients drop out of coaching. Even though we had only worked together for a month or two, they felt they didn't get the results they hired me for. I took that on myself. I thought if I was a good enough coach, they would want to stay with me longer or that I would be able to help them get results faster. You can see where the self-doubt and fear came in.

For those of us in the business of coaching, there are so many things in how we've been taught regarding how to grow a business that automatically set us up to experience self-doubt and fear. I have found that three specific mind-sets are at the root of many of the self-doubts and fears that coaches experience.

Three Mind-Sets That Trigger Self-Doubt and Fear in Coaches

1. I have to have done it myself before I can help someone else. I believe coaching is the solution to anything, that it can help anyone solve any problem, and that it is the most powerful force for change on earth. Coaches can help people who are single get into a relationship, they can help people start and grow a business, or they can help people lose weight. Coaches can help anyone do pretty much anything.

It's a specific skill set that allows coaches to do all of this, but we get it into our heads somehow that we have to have achieved it ourselves first. We can't be fifteen pounds overweight. We can't be single. We can't be in debt. In order to be a great coach, we all need to be totally sexy millionaires with 0% body fat and thriving in great relationships in which we never fight or argue.

Logically we all know that's not true, but somewhere deep inside it's in there anyway. We have doubts and insecurities. Maybe we think, *I don't need to be totally perfect, but I can't be struggling to grow my business if I'm trying to help other people grow their businesses.* These thoughts and doubts and fears are in there, and they sabotage us.

2. If I offer a sample session in order to get clients, and if I'm a great coach, people will hire me. Sample sessions don't work well for getting clients. We think, *If I do a sample session, people* *will see how great of a coach I am.* But along with that, we also think, *If people aren't hiring me after a sample session, that must mean I'm not a good coach.* Do you see the twisted, reverse logic in those statements?

The truth is that sample sessions aren't a great way to get clients. If you do lots of sample sessions thinking people will hire you, and then if they don't hire you, you start thinking you're not a good coach.

3. Allowing clients to sign up on a month-to-month or short-term basis will help me get more clients. A lot of coaching schools will recommend that you let clients sign up on a month-to-month basis so that you have no long-term plan or agreement requiring a client to work with you for six months or a year. They also suggest that you sign clients up for just three months at a time.

The problem here is that most clients are going to take a long time to see results. If someone wants to lose sixty pounds, they're not going to accomplish that during a sample session. They're also not going to lose sixty pounds in your first month of coaching no matter good you are, no matter how good their diet is, and no matter how much they exercise. They're just not going to lose all sixty pounds in thirty days.

It's important that clients sign up for six months or a year at a time; however, because we aren't taught that going in, what happens is we don't set an expectation with clients that they need to work with us for that long. Because of that, clients don't stick around.

They might hire you and continue as a client for one, two, or even three months. In the early days, my client-retention rate was right around ninety days. I was continually looking for more clients, and it made me doubt myself. I would ask myself, "Why do these clients keep dropping out? Why aren't they getting the results they wanted?" And then I would assume that the reason was because I was not a good enough coach.

These three things were triggering a lot of self-doubt and fear, so I had to figure out what I could do to work through them. I studied everything from neurolinguistic programming (NLP) to hypnotherapy to the use of technology in coaching. There are actually devices out there to help you experience a breakthrough.

I tried anything and everything to work through my self-doubt, fear, and limiting beliefs. A lot of the techniques out there really do work. Ultimately I settled on just a few techniques that I use consistently for myself in order to achieve breakthroughs.

I have an entire coach training program which covers five areas I coach people on in general. Every coach probably works on some of these five things, but I recommend that coaches learn how to do all five.

Five Areas Coaches Should Focus On With Their Clients

1. **Clarify** their direction.
2. **Strategize** their actions.
3. **Upgrade** their skills.
4. **Optimize** their environment.
5. **Master** their psychology.

In my Rapid Coaching Academy Coach Training Program, I help people to overcome self-doubt. There are a lot of techniques that will help someone change their thoughts. It sounds simple: If you're thinking *this*, don't think that. Start thinking *this* instead. The problem is that a lot of these things are nonverbal—or not even intellectual—thoughts; they're just feelings we have—emotions.

We are all works in progress. We're all growing and we're all working to achieve new goals. Even though I hit a million dollars last year in sales, I'm still growing my business. There are still challenges. Between adding people to my team and having a baby, there are obviously new challenges I'm working through. There's always more to work on, which is one reason why we definitely don't need to be perfect ourselves in order to coach clients. No one is perfect.

I use the Emotional Reintegration Technique to help me resolve issues as they come up. The things we resist are usually related to emotional feelings; all of our fears are fears of feeling. Everything we're afraid of—whether it's getting hit by a bus or heights or public speaking—stems from a feeling. We're afraid of how we would *feel* if what we fear actually happened.

All feelings are either physical or emotional. A fear of heights is actually a fear of falling and dying and of what the pain might feel like, both physically and emotionally. A fear of public speaking is actually a fear of feeling humiliated or embarrassed or rejected. All fears are fears of feeling.

"The things we resist are usually related to emotional feelings; all of our fears are fears of feeling. We're afraid of how we would feel if what we fear actually happened."

Four Steps of Emotional Reintegration

Step 1: Notice the Feeling
In starting to work through fears and doubts, what I recommend is to invite a specific feeling to come up rather than to do what we normally do when we feel something we don't like to feel, which is to push it away or distract ourselves with TV or beer or chocolate or whatever it is. Invite that feeling in and notice where in your body the feeling is the strongest. Just take notice.

For example, when I think about going to a networking event in order to find clients, I feel a sense of dread or insecurity. I think, *I know I need to go out and speak to grow my business, but I'm afraid people are going to think that I'm just trying to sell stuff.* This same thought process takes place in whatever is holding someone back. Maybe someone wants to try dating, but when they think about talking to someone they find attractive or are interested in, they feel tension in their chest. Maybe someone wants to lose weight, but when they think about going to a gym to exercise, they experience a feeling of dread. Whatever it is, get in touch with that feeling and notice where the feeling is located in the body.

The first step is just to notice the feeling, because feelings live somewhere in the body. It might be in your chest, your stomach, your throat, or your head. It could be anywhere. Just be attentive to whatever is going on in your body.

Step 2: Locate the Feeling and Focus Your Attention There
Once you notice where the feeling is most intense, the second step is to focus your attention on that area. If the feeling is in your chest, notice that and pinpoint the most intense spot. Then focus your attention there.

Step 3: Accept the Feeling Unconditionally
You can't just grit your teeth and go through these motions in order to make the feeling go away. You have to be unconditionally accepting or even loving of that feeling.

A lot of people say, "I don't love that feeling. I hate the way that feels." Maybe so, but what is important is to love and accept the feeling unconditionally for a few moments without trying to analyze it or make it go away. If you start feeling the feeling and it starts your mind racing, just gently turn your attention back to the feeling and be present to it.

Think of it like a crying baby. Part of you probably wants to put the baby in the other room, close the door, go downstairs, and turn on the TV or grab a piece of pizza just to tune out and not have to deal with it. While there's one part of you that may want to do that, there's another part that knows that baby needs something. It might need food, a diaper, or just to be held. In the same way, you have to invite your feelings in instead of putting them aside and trying to get as far away from them as you can. You have to open up and simply be present with your feelings.

Step 4: Notice What's Happening and Follow the Feeling
Notice what's happening with the feeling. It might stay the same. It might expand or contract and tighten up. It might move from your chest up to your throat. It might snake around your body a little bit. Whatever it does, follow the feeling wherever it goes until there's nothing left.

This process can take a few seconds or a few minutes. Sometimes it can even take several hours, although this is rare. When it does take several hours, you don't have to be present with it for that entire block of time all at once. Be present to it for a little while and then, if you need to, go do something else. Come back to it at another time. In my experience, only 10% or 20% of the time does it take long, focused, or even multiple sessions. Most of the time it just takes a few moments minutes for the shift to occur.

Once the feeling seems to have run its course and you return to a place of peace, think about the original situation again and see if it brings something up again. If it does, then run through the process again. If it doesn't, then you pretty much have the whole thing solved. Your self-doubts and fears can be gone in just a few moments.

The ultimate proof is usually in the pudding. If you have a fear of public speaking and you work through it to the point where you feel peaceful when you think about public speaking, then what you need to do is to actually put yourself in that situation and make sure that it's completely resolved. Most of the time—probably 90% to 95% of the time—it is completely resolved. It's only maybe 5% of the time that you might notice some other feelings coming up. But even if you do, they are usually not nearly as intense as they were before, so just repeat the process again until they're gone.

It usually only takes a few seconds to a few minutes to resolve something that, for many people, has been a challenge for them their whole life. It *can* be resolved in just a few moments, and then you will never have that issue again. It's very powerful.

I: That is powerful. What are your best secrets for acquiring more coaching clients?

CM: Well, I shared about my journey, the challenges I went through, and how I have grown my business over the last ten years, including the early days of struggling. Last year I grew my business to over a million dollars, and I'd love to share some techniques to help coaches get clients and grow their business fast. There are three fast-acting strategies for getting clients that I'll go ahead and share; these are three of my best ideas.

Often people try so many different techniques to get clients. They blog, utilize Facebook, write a book, network, tweet, and basically spread themselves thin in an attempt to grow their business. Meanwhile, it isn't really paying off, or at least not very quickly. I want to simplify and clarify that process.

Top Three Strategies for Getting Coaching Clients

1. Let potential clients know about you. There are a lot of marketing strategies you can employ to let potential clients hear about you, including advertising, networking, article marketing, etc. There are a lot of options, but I'm going to assume that most people already know what these options include. Then there's the actual *doing* of those things and of course secrets for how to make those efforts pay off.

2. Bring clients in for an introductory session. A lot of people don't realize that clients need to have an intro session with you. I mentioned earlier that sample sessions don't work very well, so you actually want to do something different in your intro sessions, and I'll explain more about that in a moment.

A lot of coaches list their coaching fees on their Web site and are out there busting their butts in the hopes that people will somehow hear about them. Then they just wait for people to call and hire them. Even if they do offer an intro session, it's not a very enticing offer. They just offer a free, no-obligation coaching session, and to be honest, that's not very enticing.

I recommend that you make the intro session more compelling and that you send out your intro session offer to your e-mail list, at networking events, and during public speaking presentations so that you get a rush of people wanting to have a session with you right away.

I go into this in more depth in my program, *Free Sessions That Sell*. Instead of just saying, "I offer a no-obligation coaching session," you want to make your sessions enticing. For example, if you are a relationship coach, offer a thirty-minute "Find Your Soul Mate Now" coaching session during which you work with the client to create a crystal clear vision of the kind of person they would like to date and the kind of relationship they would like to have with that person. Advertise that you will uncover hidden challenges that may be sabotaging their success with when it comes to dating. Emphasize that the client will leave the session renewed, refreshed, and inspired to attract the person of their dreams once and for all.

Make your intro session compelling and then send it out via your e-mail list or however you can. Tell people they can have one of these sessions with you for a limited time and that you have a few sessions available. Be prepared. You could get a mad rush of people wanting to have an intro session with you, and through that you could get a lot of clients. You could fill up your practice in a matter of a week or two if you have an e-mail list ready to go. If you don't, you could get a bunch of clients just from people you know.

On my main Web site, I give away prewritten intro session offers. I have ten of them available, so if you're a relationship coach, you can pick up the relationship coach template, or if you're a business coach, you can pick up the business coach template. You can easily copy and paste the template text into an e-mail and send it to your list or to your friends and family in order to entice people to want to have an intro session with you. From there you can get them to sign up for coaching in order to help them to make the changes they want to make.

3. Have a powerful process in place so that people want to sign up. One of the things I teach in *Free Sessions That Sell* is a step-by-step process that you can lead people through so that you're not doing sample sessions anymore. Again, sample sessions work a little bit to get clients, but not very well. If you're charging $195 a month for coaching with no long-term commitment like I was when I first started, then sample sessions will work great. Maybe 15% to 20% of the people I had intro sessions with actually hired me.

But if you use the process I teach in *Free Sessions That Sell*, you can get anywhere between 20% (on the low end) and 80% to 90% (on the high end) of the people you have intro sessions with to hire you, and your coaching fees can be much, much higher. As I mentioned, my coaching fee these days is $9,500 a month, and just doing a sample session would definitely not get people to sign up for a year of coaching at that cost.

How to Format Your Intro Sessions to Get Hired
- Help the client clarify what they want and what it would mean for them to have it.
- Help the client uncover challenges that are keeping them from moving forward and to see how those challenges are costing them in their lives, both and financially and emotionally.
- Show the client how what you do as a coach is going to help them overcome their challenges and achieve their goals.

If you can do these things in your intro session process, you're going to get a very high percentage of people who want to hire you based on those sessions.

I: What inspires you, Christian?

CM: Personal growth and spiritual growth inspire me as well as those who teach and lead in those areas. I recently saw don Miguel Ruiz, author of *The Four Agreements, The Mastery of Love, The Voice of Knowledge,* and co-author of *The Fifth Agreement* with his son, don Jose Ruiz. They spoke for two hours, and it was just awesome stuff.

I'm a big fan of Dan Millman, who wrote *Way of the Peaceful Warrior*—which was made into the movie *Peaceful Warrior*—as well as many other books, and I actually had the good fortune of having him guest speak along with me at my last live event. He inspires me. Another person who inspires me is David Hawkins, author of

Power vs Force and many other books.

Those people inspire me as well as anyone who wants to help other people. Coaches inspire me. People who really care inspire me. People who have the courage to go for it in their business and who want to make the world a better place inspire me. Basically, people who are passionate inspire me.

As far as where *my* inspiration comes from, ideas come from everywhere for what I end up doing and what programs I create. But I do believe my inspiration is divine inspiration.

"You might be thinking, I don't know where my calling is. I don't know where I should go. Just keep putting one foot in front of the other. The path will unfold. It doesn't always reveal itself all at once."

I: What made you choose this arena for your life's great work?

CM: You know what, I feel like it chose me; I didn't pick this path, this path picked me. I don't know that I could do anything else even if I wanted to. I was meant to do it. I felt called to be out there helping coaches in this way. So I just keep following wherever I'm called to go, and I keep doing what feels right and what feels fun.

It wasn't like I heard a voice telling me, "Go lead the coaching industry." I definitely got the thought in my head at some point to become a leader of the coaching industry, and it felt really exciting, but most of it came in small chunks. You might be thinking, *I don't know where my calling is. I don't know where I should go.* Just keep putting one foot in front of the other. The path will unfold. It doesn't always reveal itself all at once.

Chapter
6

The Science of Getting the
Results You Want
Dr. Sherry Buffington

Chapter 6
The Science of Getting the Results You Want
Dr. Sherry Buffington

Dr. Sherry Buffington has been immersed in the study of human nature, motivation, and success principles since 1978 and is a top expert on behaviors and motivations. She is the founder, President, and CEO of NaviCore International, Inc., a research and development firm focused on personal and professional development, motivation, and effectiveness. NaviCore International, Inc. is a pioneer in the field of developmental assessments and personal effectiveness.

Sherry is a coach, consultant, trainer, presenter, and the author of several books, including *The Law of Abundance* which provides a scientific perspective on the way energy impacts the outcomes of life, work, and relationships for all people all the time. It provides answers to the questions many of us have as to why we don't get the results we want.

I: The title of your book, *The Law of Abundance,* implies that there is a law that guarantees abundance. Do you believe that's true?

SB: Absolutely! The Law of Abundance is a universal law that *never* fails. When all of the elements are in place, it is as precise and predictable as the law that allows us to have electricity in our homes.

I had been studying success principles for years and didn't really understand how powerfully our choices affect our outcomes until I discovered how the laws that govern energy impact humanity. These laws go far beyond positive thinking Law of Attraction principles as they are typically presented. What is presented as the Law of

Attraction is really just one part of a seven-part formula.

I: There are a ton of books out there about success and prosperity. What's different about yours?

SB: *The Law of Abundance* lays out the entire formula, defines and describes all seven parts, and presents them in a way that allows them to be tested and proven, both scientifically and in our lives on every level, from personal to global. *The Law of Abundance* is not just a philosophy; it is based on pure science. Every principle laid out in the book has been proven and tested in myriad ways and every one works without fail.

The testing of this science started when Benjamin Franklin discovered we could harness energy. With that awareness, physicists began studying precisely how harnessed energy works, and they uncovered the unfailing laws that we now use to power our world. We have automobiles, airplanes, toasters, refrigerators, homes that are lighted and climate controlled, and all sorts of conveniences because those unfailing laws were discovered and put to use. By understanding how *we* fit into the equation, we can get the same precise results that physicists have gotten with electricity.

In 1905, Albert Einstein proved that everything is energy. No scientist disputes that. If everything is energy, then you and I must fit into that equation, and the laws that govern energy must also apply to us—and as it turns out, they do.

When we understand how energy determines every one of our outcomes in the same precise and predictable way that it determines what an electrical appliance delivers, then we can design our own lives to express exactly what we want just as precisely and predictably.

Not knowing how to apply the laws of energy effectively is what prevents so many individuals from achieving their goals and realizing their dreams.

It is not uncommon for people to blame their poor results on a process—goal setting, for example—or on life circumstances, or on something other than the way they have designed their receiver. But like an appliance, a goal must be designed to receive and translate energy the way we intend, or what we get back will not be what we wanted. The energy we send out returns to us exactly as we have

"A goal must be designed to receive and translate energy the way we intend, or what we get back will not be what we wanted . . . We get what we create."

designed our receivers—our goals and intents—to translate it. We get what we create. So knowing precisely how we are creating what we get, and what to adjust when we are not getting exactly what we want, can dramatically alter our lives and outcomes.

I: The idea of a self-fulfilling prophecy has also been studied and proven. I know you're referring to the Law of Abundance, but aren't *The Secret* and the Law of Attraction versions of self-fulfilling prophecy?

SB: In many ways yes, because intent and belief are two ways in which we direct energy. But if we look at the laws of energy and how we fit into those laws, we see that there is much more to how we manage energy than just our thoughts and beliefs.

Energy flows naturally toward an abundance of the things we desire if we don't interfere with it. Our thoughts, beliefs, and intent can boost energy toward what we want, or they can greatly interfere with it, depending on how we use them. I called my book *The Law of Abundance* and not *The Law of Energy* because energy is the *cause*, abundance is the *effect*; it is the effect we seek, but to get to the effect, we must know how to manage the cause.

The Law of Abundance *guarantees* abundance, but it does not guarantee *what* we will have an abundance of. Far too many people have an abundance of things they do *not* want as a result of misusing the laws of energy. Just as electricity naturally flows in one direction, but can be reversed, slowed, and even stopped, so too can energy in the human experience. We alter energy every time we turn lights on and off or dim them using a rheostat.

The same is true in our lives. We are always directing energy. Our on-off switch is *choice*. Our decision to do or not do is what directs our energy and determines our outcomes. Our rheostat is attitude, which evolves from our thoughts and beliefs. The more resistant our thoughts and beliefs are, the more we slow the flow of energy and prevent positive outcomes. The natural flow of energy for humans is toward the things we desire: happiness, love, contentment, freedom, prosperity—all the things we want. The fact that we desire those things and resist the opposite is proof enough that the natural flow for us is toward what we find desirable, yet that is often not our experience because we are not using the laws of energy properly.

If we just apply one part of the formula, as happens when we get too focused on typical Law of Attraction principles, we will not get the results we want. The few people that get consistent results from applying Law of Attraction principles get those results because they have the other six parts already in place whether they know it or not. For these people, the only thing missing is receptivity, and that is what the Law of Attraction encourages. If receptivity was all that was missing from the abundance formula, the minute an individual with all the other pieces in place became more receptive, energy would begin to flow, and that could become a "self-fulfilling prophecy," so to speak.

If you look at the energy cycle as a circuit—which it is in all harnessed systems, and we are harnessed energy just as electricity is—you can see that it flows as a result of the circuit being complete. The Law of Attraction addresses just one part of the circuit—the return line. The Law of Abundance presents the entire circuit with all seven parts, and all seven are essential.

I: What happens when one or more of these elements is missing?

SB: When any part of the formula is missing, we do not and cannot get the results we want in full measure. The problem for most is in not knowing what's wrong when we don't get the results. When we can't see what needs to be adjusted, everything is hit and miss. If we don't know what the formula for abundance looks like or what parts of the formula we are misapplying, we can't know how or why we are getting the results we get, so we don't have the means to make purposeful adjustments. When we can see the entire picture and know exactly what is preventing us from getting the results we want, we can make the necessary adjustments and get the intended results.

I: Are you saying that if all of the elements are in place, the law is infallible and always leads to more of what we want? Don't some things—sometimes negative experiences—just happen to us that are beyond our control?

SB: Certainly, and the reason is because life is an open system. In an open system all things impact all other things. To assume that we are fully responsible for every outcome is foolish. That notion completely discounts the reality of an open system which is the only system in which life can exist. Without an open system life would eventually disappear like a battery running down.

A dead battery is a closed system in which energy has reached equilibrium. Energy is always seeking equilibrium, and when it reaches it, energy ceases to flow. In a dead battery, energy is balanced and has ceased to flow. In people, equilibrium is the state of total contentment—complete satisfaction—and, while we seek that, if we ever actually reached it, death would not be far behind. If we remained completely satisfied, we would have no incentive to do anything. At complete equilibrium there is no further movement. It's the introduction of discomfort and challenges and imbalances that produces action, and action is the essence of life.

We don't want our life to look like a dead battery. Life as an open system is dynamic, and in an open, dynamic system, all things impact one another—what happens in nature will impact us, and what one person does will impact another.

We can't prevent challenging occurrences, but when we understand the Law of Abundance—how it works—and know how to work *with* it, we are better prepared for things that are out of our control.

I: In your book, you state that most people lack self-awareness because, as children, they began masking their truth to meet expectations. How do we know if we're wearing a mask?

SB: Look at your level of satisfaction with *self*—not with the world around you, but with your personal self. If you are not completely delighted with who you are—not *where* you are or *what* you are doing, but with *who you are*—then you are not living true to yourself. Every person I have ever met that is living authentically *loves* who they are. I have experienced this shift myself and have helped thousands of people over the years discover and claim their authentic self. When they do, there is always a profound shift toward joy in being who they are. Some people shift within hours, and the shift is so dramatic that, when it happens in a group setting, everyone in the room can see the change.

Virtually everyone can learn to live effectively and joyously from their authentic self, but first we have to get to that place. You can bet money that people who are not completely happy with who they are—those who are not satisfied and comfortable in their own skin—

are living someone else's idea of who they should be rather than their own authentic life.

I speak from first-hand experience and from witnessing it in others when I say that complete transformation absolutely does occur, sometimes instantly, and it is from this transformed, authentic place that we experience true abundance. I conducted a fifteen-year-long study to determine what leads to success and what prevents it. Of the essential qualities I uncovered, authentic self-awareness tops the list. None of the other qualities develop fully without that one.

Whether we are looking at our overall results or our personal satisfaction, awareness is key. If we aren't aware of the laws that determine our every outcome so that we can work with them effectively, we don't get what we want in the external world. If we aren't aware of our authentic self so we can walk our own unique path, we don't get what we want in our internal world. Ultimately, the internal and external are all about living authentically, and to do that, we have to be aware of the elements that result in an authentic life.

Chapter
7

Get Social and Get Rich
Viki Winterton

Chapter 7
Get Social and Get Rich
Viki Winterton

Viki Winterton is a respected coach and consultant who has practiced since 1989 for Fortune 100 companies and many individuals. Her successful twenty-two-year career in coaching, change management, process re-engineering, advertising, and business development has garnered rave reviews and successful results in domestic and international settings for a wide variety of industries.

Viki is the founder of Expert Insights Family of Opportunity including Expert Insights Publishing; *Insights* and *PUBLISHED!* magazines; The Coach Exchange; and Write Away, Write Now! social networks and broadcast with over 9200 active international members and 20,000 subscribers. She is also co-founder of The Coaches' Edge Extravaganza.

I: I understand you live half of each year in Mexico but you started your career in the U.S.?

VW: Yes. I actually started my career when I was in my mid-twenties. I founded an ad agency, and that opened the door for many wonderful things that unfolded in such an amazing fashion for me over the next few decades.

I: You have been coaching teams of individuals within Fortune 100 companies since coaching began as an industry. How did that transpire?

VW: Basically, our ad agency was tremendously successful, and we were acquired after three years. Some of my Fortune 100 client companies actually engaged me to come and work for them directly to be involved with change management and process re-engineering, so I began coaching teams in that process.

It was fascinating work, and I did that for over twenty years in some of the most unbelievable locations in the world with amazing people and incredible companies. Because I was traveling about 95% of the time during many of those years, I felt isolated even from others in coaching. I went, did the job, and there wasn't much time left over for being able to network or connect with my peers in the industry the way I wanted to.

I founded The Coach Exchange—a network of coaches—about three and a half years ago. It was designed to help coaches and solo entrepreneurs connect and communicate on equal footing and to provide them with access to people at any level in order to learn and exchange ideas. It was available for everyone, whether they were just starting in their business or if they were extremely experienced and considered a household name.

Just in the past year and a half, other companies have spring-boarded from that one. We started incorporating live events, publishing opportunities, broadcast opportunities, and so forth. These were all created for coaches, solo entrepreneurs, and small business owners—both women and men—to provide an outlet for showcasing their talents alongside household names and visionaries in their field.

I: I love this idea. As a business owner myself, I know from experience that it can be lonely when first starting out. But you have built something that allows solopreneurs and coaches to connect with one another and to feel like part of a community or movement. That's powerful.

You started by owning your own ad agency which was wildly successful and then moved into doing team and one-on-one coaching with Fortune 100 companies. From there you launched The Coach Exchange. As far as business backgrounds go, yours is pretty extensive. In your experience, does someone need that level of experience to create a successful Web business?

VW: The most important ingredients anyone can have when approaching a business are a clear vision, a passion for what you want to do, and a true entrepreneurial spirit.

When I founded my ad agency in my mid-twenties, I had no idea how to do any of the things that needed to be done in order to make it happen. While it's true that there are resources available and you can find ways to learn what you need to know, you can never replace passion—that spirit that drives an entrepreneur so strongly that nothing can stop them. That's what gets you through challenges and times of learning when it comes to growth. That spirit—that passion—will get you through, and it will move you toward success.

To me, the learning part is important, but it is almost a technicality. Those other ingredients really have to be there. If you're new to business or venturing into a new arena, that driving fire, passion, and entrepreneurial spirit is the biggest asset you can possibly have.

I: I love that you mentioned challenging times, because that's life and business. There are going to be times when you are facing tough challenges, and it is important to be resilient and to look at those challenges as learning opportunities as you tap into other resources as you mentioned.

VW: It brings to mind a really interesting conversation I had with one of our coaches. He is a performance coach to world-class athletes, CEOs, and people in powerful leadership roles.

He said one of the things he's found that distinguishes those who achieve in high-visibility positions or high-performance athletic roles is the way they perceive challenges. They perceive them as part of the process. They don't respond with fear and they don't view them negatively. Instead, they consider them part of the growth process for attaining maximum performance capacity. I thought that was fascinating.

The talent has to be there, the learning has to take place, and the tools need to be made available, but perception can make all the difference between success and failure.

I: One of the most powerful things one of my coaches ever said to me was, "Are you managing your perceptions?" I thought, *How interesting. Am I just letting my mind run away, or am I actually managing my perception of what's going on in my life?* I love the idea of managing perceptions.

VW: Isn't it powerful to know that we have the capacity to determine what we think about anything and everything? We can know something in theory, but we might not always live it.

I: I'd like to discuss the idea of a woman's innate social wisdom. One of the things you stand behind is the concept that women have a natural advantage in using social media, which we know is one of the best ways to spread the word about what is going on in one's business. Why do you think women have a natural edge when it comes to using social media to achieve success?

VW: It's interesting because I coached over the course of a few decades in Fortune 100 companies to Fortune 500 companies. Some of these companies were very large, and I started to notice that when technology really came to the forefront, the executive teams I was working with were having some challenges working in a team environment. It wasn't due to a lack of desire; it seemed like foreign territory to them.

When technology advanced, all of a sudden e-mails became shorter and more succinct. It almost became a style of doing business to have short snippets of communication in general. Along with this change came a challenge for people to really communicate on all levels in a business environment and to really get to know each other. I found that I needed to guide them toward a consensus when it came to really important issues for their company; it was becoming more difficult, not because of a lack of willingness to do so on their part, but just because they weren't used to it.

To me, it's very natural that social networks have come up, because it's like a pendulum. Things swayed toward efficiency and the technical components and the communication got lost, and now things are swinging back toward networks, which are a powerful form of developing communication. This type of communication comes naturally to women.

I noticed in working with The Coach Exchange and Write Away, Write Now! as well as a number of other networks including Facebook, LinkedIn, and YouTube that it's important to bring more of yourself to the table than just your business. It's about you and who you are. It's about how you handle a flat tire on your way to an important meeting. People want to get to know you and what you're doing in various aspects of your life. They want that in-depth experience, and I think women are better equipped to deliver that than men are. It's not that men can't bring these things to social media too, but it's almost a natural thing for women to bring their whole selves to that forum.

"It's important to bring more of yourself to the table than just your business. It's about who you are. People want that in-depth experience, and I think women are better equipped to deliver that."

In small business, we all have a tremendous advantage today. When I started out in advertising many decades ago, all promotion had a price tag; PR, advertising, broadcast time—everything was paid for. Now you have access to all of this wonderful free exposure through the Web and technology. It's extraordinary that you can use it to its maximum capacity at no cost to you.

I: I agree. I believe fundamentally in feminine growth through connection. We love to get together and talk. That's just our nature. However, it's more than that; the female brain is actually wired to be more social and to connect in that way. That's not to say that men who don't have those skills can't develop them, but women are physiologically hardwired to be social.

You have a free forum going in what you offer. How does this expand one's influence?

VW: There is a saying I've heard since I've been in business: "People do business with people they like." Women are naturally inclined to evoke an emotional charge to want to do business, to want to make a change, and to want to move forward. This is inherent in our nature, and it's a wonderful thing because it lends itself so well to social media and to networking opportunities.

I: Having mastered this modality, where would you recommend someone start if they are new to social media?

VW: First, I would suggest you start with what you want. The most important thing is to clearly define what you want, what you feel passionate about, your personal vision, and what that looks like for you.

It's important not to place the marketing research of what will sell or what people are looking to buy ahead of everything else. It's more important to understand where your passion lies and where your unique message comes in. How can you provide what people are looking for in your own unique way? You need to become very clear about your message.

You need to start by asking yourself three questions:
- What do I love to do?
- Where do I love to play?
- Who do I love to play with?

It's basically about asking yourself, "Where do I find the fun?" That's what ignites your passion, and that's what's going to carry you through those learning periods in business that we all experience. Regardless of how successful you are as your business grows, there are always going to be new things that crop up that you need to learn in order to create the success you want. To look at that in such a way that you're inviting it in will only happen if you really love what you're doing.

A lot of people talk about market research. To me, this is simpler. It is basically just learning more about the people I love working with and who I love doing things for. It's about creating new things they can benefit from. By learning more about what they like, I'm learning more about that which I love. That doesn't sound nearly as daunting as having to do competitive analysis or market research. It all needs to start with what you love, because then you'll love playing there, you'll love spending time there, and the time will fly.

I sometimes work remotely in Mexico, and I'll get up from my work and I'll think, *Oh my gosh! It's noon and I forgot to brush my teeth because I'm so engrossed in what's been happening since I got up at 7:00 this morning*. The time flies by. It feels like it's only been minutes when in reality it's been hours. That only happens when you're doing what you love.

The second thing I would suggest is to discover the *essence* of what you love. I've done a number of different things, and even now I'm involved in publishing, broadcasting, networking, and so forth. That may sound like it's all somewhat diverse, but when I sat down and really analyzed the essence of what I love to do, I realized that it has remained consistent my whole life.

The essence of what I love to do is to represent people and to bring resources and those who need those resources together. That is where I really shine and it's what I love to do. Although I'm on stage and interviewed often, that's not my goal. My goal is to find the stage, find the people who need to be on that stage, provide the audience, and then bring all of those components together.

When I realized the true essence of what I love to do, it changed everything. Now I understand that when something falls outside of that arena, it's not where my passion really lies. I'm able to look at that criteria and turn away from things that may not be as rewarding for me personally as other things would be.

I: Traditionally in marketing and advertising you have a PR person, but you're kind of an RP instead; you represent people and provide them with the opportunity to offer their gifts to those who need them.

VW: Yes. Often when people are talking about finding their true purpose, it can get confusing, because they're looking at events or positions they've held and trying to string those different things together. It's really more about the essence. If you narrow it down to how those things led you to be of service in the world, then the essence will surface.

I: Let's talk about this powerful presence, which obviously you've been able to create, as well as developing a loyal following on the Web. How do you manifest this quickly?

VW: There are six tips I follow in everything I do. They have served me well, and I hope they will serve others well too.

Six Tips for Creating a Powerful Presence and a Loyal Following

1. Determine Who You Want to Serve
As I mentioned earlier, you probably know where you like to play or can determine what that looks like. So who do you want to play with?

Some of the things you need to determine—and the Web is fantastic for this kind of research—are things such as their characteristics, what they're like, if they make a certain amount of money if that is important to your vision, and whether they share a common geographic location. That last one was especially key for me when I decided to change to a Web-based business. I knew there needed to be no geographic limitations.

2. Decide on the Ideal Size of Your Market
My market is fairly broad because it is important for coaches and

solo entrepreneurs to have global access. You may feel strongly about doing something within your hometown, your state, a specific country, or a certain demographic.

3. Locate Your Market
Find out where your market is located including within specific organizations. For example, we work closely with the International Coach Federation, and forming that relationship helped us establish ourselves in the beginning as a network.

Find out what organizations, churches, associations, and so forth your target market gravitates to. Not only can you access your market through personal involvement in those organizations, but you can tap into them through groups all over the Web.

4. Find Out What Publications They Read and What Web Sites They Visit
What are their issues? Where are the forums for those issues that they all have in common? How can you contribute while building your reputation and expertise as one who can solve their problems?

5. Identify What Social Media They Use
By identifying specific social media targets they use, you can get involved in actually communicating with them and setting yourself up as an expert almost overnight.

When you're looking at social media and the Web, it can be overwhelming, particularly if you're just starting out. The most important places for you to have a presence are on LinkedIn, Facebook, Twitter, and YouTube. You need to have at least one network presence within the industry that you are serving. Wherever you choose to be of service, you need to start developing some visibility in that industry or that venue, and there are a number of ways to do that on the Web that are easy to use and very powerful. Keep it simple if you're just starting out.

If you are thinking of starting your own community, LinkedIn, Facebook, and many niche networks offer groups that you can start for free with easy setup, and you can start gaining recognition as an expert almost instantly.

The most important tools I use for connecting and posting on the Web are Ping.fm, Seesmic.com, and SocialOomph.com. In addition, Fiverr.com offers a multitude of Web services for five dollars or less.

6. Learn About Your Market

There are some things you need to learn about your market in order to determine if your product or service is a good fit or design and if it will answer the most critical needs of your market.

What You Need to Learn About Your Market

- **What do they want?** What do they feel they can't live without?
- **What are they talking about?** This is so important and it shifts quickly. Discover how they want to receive information, products, and services from you. It changes as rapidly as technology, so it's very important to be able to tap into what they're talking about *now* and what's most important to them.
- **What do they find exciting and interesting and what are their biggest problems?** Addressing these two areas in a very specific and unique way will be your formula for success in regards to what you offer.
- **What are their dreams? What do they aspire to?** What—at their very highest level—do they see for themselves? Getting in touch with this can be the most important thing to understand about anyone you're providing a product or service for.
- **What do they need? What keeps them up at night?** It's important to be able to understand what their most pressing needs are. It's also important to be able to speak to them authentically in their language. The service, the product, the need, and the message always have to resonate with authenticity.

One tool I've used frequently is surveys. Once I've determined that I'm going to start a new business or project such as a publication, broadcast, or live event, I'll put out a survey. Even with all of my research, I may not have an absolute understanding of what my market is looking for. Survey Monkey is an excellent free tool. It's all about communication. If you want to serve a specific community, why not ask them what they want?

The most wonderful thing about this is that you can come back to them and say, "We heard you. This is what you said you wanted, and that is the reason why we designed what we're offering in this way. We heard you and we have an answer to your critical problem or need that's specific to what you asked for."

Once the survey is complete, the next step is to clarify your message. How can you strike an emotional chord while maintaining authenticity and at the same time use everything you've learned in order to create a fabulous message that will move people emotionally to want to work with you? It's a matter of being able to lay out the benefits in a delivery method that's fun and resonates with you. Perhaps you have a book in you, you want to establish a network, or maybe you prefer broadcast or blogging. It can and should be effective and enjoyable!

I: How important is it to collaborate and joint venture with other people, and how do you attract potential joint venture partners who can support you?

VW: Joint venturing is a matter of developing a relationship with people you care about and admire. It's about so much more than numbers, the size of someone's mailing list, or how much exposure you will get. Those things are good business practices and good things to consider, but the most important consideration is, *What do I think of this person? Do I admire their work?*

> *"'Follow your bliss.' I believe life is too short to do anything else."*

If you can honestly say, "I am approaching this person because I really want to develop a relationship with them and I admire what they're doing," and that comes from an authentic feeling, chances are—if they say yes—the experience is going to be amazing. From there it can open up opportunities for you to create more work together. We have developed great relationships this way for our networks, events, and publications with many people I never thought I would even meet. It's truly magical.

I: Viki, what final message do you have for readers? What words of inspiration or encouragement would you like them to walk away with today?

VW: I'd like to share a quote by Joseph Campbell; it's my favorite. It's simply says, "Follow your bliss." I believe life is just too short to do anything else.

Chapter
8

Discover What It Means to Become Spotlightworthy
Tsufit

Chapter 8
Discover What It Means to Become Spotlightworthy
Tsufit

Tsufit is the author of the hot new book, *Step Into the Spotlight: A Guide to Getting Noticed.* Tsufit was recently featured in *Entrepreneur* magazine and has been described by *The Toronto Star* as "a starburst of energy . . . bright, bubbly, and upbeat," and by *Publisher's Weekly* as "a coaching dynamo." Her book, *Step Into the Spotlight,* has been endorsed by Tom Peters, Jay Conrad Levinson, Jack Trout, and BNI founder Dr. Ivan Misner.

As a singer, television actress, comedienne, and the subject of hundreds of featured newspaper articles and television and radio appearances, Tsufit has appeared doing standup comedy in nightclubs and on national TV and has appeared on television and film commercials internationally.

Tsufit coaches entrepreneurs, business owners, authors, speakers, and CEOs to catapult their brands and themselves into a starring role. She teaches her clients to get seen, get heard, and get noticed.

I: What do you mean when you say, "All business is show business"?

T: Show business is the business of telling stories and selling stories, and show business also understands that it can't exist without an audience. The most valuable asset for anyone in show business is to possess star qualities, and this is true for any business and for any entrepreneur, but not all entrepreneurs got the memo.

It's crowded and noisy out there in the marketplace. It's as though you're stuck on channel 632. Your prospects have a TV remote and they're flipping through the channels to see what's on. They don't start at channel 632, and you can't just hope they'll find you.

You have to figure out how to attract and hold your audience's attention—how to develop box office appeal. That's what marketing is all about. It's not enough to bake a better bagel, which I call the "bake it and they will come" theory. You have to know how to get them lined up around the corner for those bagels.

I: Tell us about your background, why you chose this arena for your life's work, and why you decided to write your book, _Step Into the Spotlight._

T: I wanted to be on stage since I was a kid, but that wasn't very practical. So I ended up becoming lawyer—a downtown litigation lawyer, Dean's list, the whole thing—until one day I had that Peggy Lee moment, an "Is that all there is?" moment. I decided it was finally my turn, and I left law for the limelight.

I left law to be a singer, an actress, and a comedienne. I had just had four baby daughters in four years, and I decided to follow my dream and become an actress. I got a few roles, I started to promote and publicize myself as an actress, and I put out a music CD.

I received a lot of publicity, and pretty soon the suits came calling; businesspeople, professionals, and entrepreneurs were asking how I managed to get all of that publicity. Without a business degree or a business background in publicity or marketing, I started coaching people in business on how to get noticed and get known. Before I knew it, I started receiving invitations to be the keynote speaker at business conferences.

I was thinking, _Why me? They've got all the experience. They've got MBAs and PhDs._ But I realized that I understood something they didn't—that all business is show business. It was kind of an epiphany. The reason I was succeeding was because I knew how to hold an audience's attention. Now I show businesses how to use show business to get business.

When I started coaching people to do this, my coaching fee started to increase and increase, and before I knew it, my hourly rate was higher than it had been as a lawyer and higher than it is for _most_ lawyers. People started asking me to write a book because not everyone could afford my fee.

So I wrote *Step Into the Spotlight: A Guide to Getting Noticed.* That way, people around the world could read it, and they didn't have to access me directly.

I: What are some important lessons businesses can learn from the world of show business?

T: There are so many things they can learn. Here are just a few:

Show Business Lessons for the Business World

The Three D's of Marketing
Don't bore them. Don't bore them. *For God's sake, don't bore them!* You can't be afraid to have fun. As David Ogilvy used to say, "You can't bore people into buying."

Choose a Character
Choose a persona before you walk onto the stage. An actor doesn't make up his role on the spot; he knows ahead of time what part he's playing. I find that businesses don't usually know what part they're playing. Someone is a coach or an accountant, but they don't really carve out a specific role within that.

Never Step Onto the Stage With a Lousy Script
I go to so many conferences where I hear so many boring speakers. Whether you're the keynote speaker or if you only have thirty seconds for your intro, you have a chance to really show what you do. If you bring a little show business into it, you'll get noticed.

Give a Great Performance
A Harvard study showed that what you say only accounts for about 7% of the impression you make on your audience. Much of the rest is based on how you say it, so you have to learn how to really command an audience's attention. Some people say that's how President Obama got into office—he knows how to hold an audience's attention.

Attract Your Audience—Don't Chase Them
I have never once received a cold call from Madonna.

There is No Show Without an Audience
If you put on a play and there's no one in the audience, there is no

show. It's the same in business, but people don't realize that. People think, *Okay, I studied for ninety-five years, I became an accountant or a lawyer or whatever, and now I'm an expert.* My definition of an expert is not someone who knows what he knows, but someone who is *known* for knowing what he knows. You have to learn how to become spotlightworthy and how to attract an audience.

> *"My definition of an expert is not someone who knows what he knows, but someone who is known for knowing what he knows. You have to learn how to become spotlightworthy and how to attract an audience."*

Personality Matters

This is something we can learn from American Idol; in one of the competitions a few years back Taylor Hicks was competing against Katharine McPhee in the final two. Katharine McPhee is beautiful, but she's dime-a-dozen beautiful. She has a beautiful voice, but it's a dime-a-dozen beautiful voice. Taylor Hicks was twenty-something with gray hair and tons of personality. He probably did not have as good a voice as Katharine, but he won because he was more entertaining and he had more personality. He even named his fan club.

I: Isn't it enough just to be good at what you do? Isn't that enough to get you business?

T: Sure, if you live in a town with a population of 413 people and you're the only accountant. But if you move to a bustling metropolis of maybe 4,013 people where there are seven accountants, all of a sudden people have a choice. Which one will they choose? They all look the same. That's when it becomes important to really stand out. It's not enough to be good. How will people know you're good?

I: How do you become your own casting director?

T: When I was a kid I used to audition for shows. Those of us who had auditioned would be thrilled when we saw the cast list and saw what roles we got; we'd be thrilled if we got a great role and disappointed if we didn't get a great role.

In business, you don't have to audition. You get to be your own casting director. You get to choose your role in the marketplace, and you never have to audition for business again. You can decide: Do you want to be Batman or Robin? (By the way, you know Robin is never going to get his own show.) You also get to choose your specific role in the marketplace.

The Mac versus PC spots are brilliant examples of this. You can watch them on YouTube, or I have them on my blog as well at www.spotlightblog.com. Apple has characterized a computer—which is usually just a gray box sitting under your desk—as a person, a character, a persona. Mac is wearing a black T-shirt. He's cool, youthful, and artistic. PC is this Charlie Brown looking guy bumbling around in a brown suit. He's fussy and complicated and uncomfortable in his own skin.

Using this technique, Apple was able to not only position themselves and cast themselves in the role of the cool computer company, but they were also able to position their opponent as being bumbling. That's an example of what you can do when you become your own casting director.

I: What is the most common mistake entrepreneurs make?

Three Common Mistakes Entrepreneurs Make

1. Wearing Two Hats: I've heard the saying, "I'm here today wearing two hats." I hate that expression. If you go to a Chamber of Commerce at 7:30 in the morning, that's what you're going to hear. "I'm here today wearing two hats." Like, "I'm a rocket scientist and I make gift baskets on the side."

It is a lack of focus, because you can't fit two hats on one head. A few years ago McDonald's started selling pizza. If you were in the mood for pizza, would you throw the gang in the car and head to McDonald's? No. Nobody would. It was a lack of focus. That's one mistake—wearing two hats.

2. Not Knowing What They're Really Selling: Even if they're only focused on selling one thing, it's usually the wrong thing. They think they're selling soup when in reality they're selling comfort. They think they're selling makeup when they're really selling confidence. Sometimes even the big boys get it wrong.

Quite a few years ago, Coca-Cola got distracted by Pepsi and began thinking they were selling taste. Pepsi did the Pepsi Challenge, and everyone said they liked the taste of Pepsi better than Coke. So Coke made a new drink that people in blind taste tests said they liked better than Pepsi *or* Coke—they called it New Coke.

The result was the biggest marketing fiasco in history. It bombed. It tanked. They had to pull it off the shelves. Why? Coke forgot what they were really selling. Coke was "the real thing." Coke was the American dream in a bottle—that's what Roger Enrico, former CEO of Pepsi, said about his competitor, Coke. Coke forgot that it was "the real thing." You've got to know what you're really selling.

3. Suffering From Professionalitis: Accountants, corporate executives, coaches—they all look the same, sound the same, and speak the same corporate gobbledygook or coach-speak with phrases like "break through the barriers." They're interchangeable. They focus too much on appearing professional and way too little on showing their brand's personality.

Business has so many rules. In show business, the only rule is you've got to break all the rules.

I: What does character development mean, and how can it help you develop your brand?

T: If you were cast in a role in a movie or a TV show, you'd be asking yourself or the director, "What does this character look like? What does this character sound like? What does he say and how does he say it? What is his backstory? What led him to where he is today?"

There's a joke in theater: The actor asks his director, "What's my motivation?" The director responds, "To get paid." In business, that's the real answer. There are all kinds of questions that business owners and branding specialists should be asking themselves. You have to ask yourself, "What is my distinct persona in the marketplace? What is my distinct character?"

For example, Al Pacino and Richard Simmons would never be up for the same part in a movie—never. Can you image Al Pacino sweating to the oldies? No. You've got to develop a character.

Henry Winkler played Fonzie on the hit show *Happy Days*. Henry Winkler was supposed to be a bit part, but he added huge amounts of flavor and character. He was originally wearing a cotton jacket. He changed to a black leather jacket. He had this "I'm no choir boy" kind of attitude. All of a sudden it resonated, and Fonzie became such a star that they wanted to rename the show *Fonzie's Happy Days*. He was humble enough to say, "Don't do that." It's the same thing Johnny Cash did with his persona. And it can help you develop a brand.

You also have to pay attention to the *continuity* of your brand. For example, Unilever has been accused of lack of continuity in regards to its brand because it sells Dove, which is all about a Campaign for Real Beauty and The Beauty Within, etc. But they're the same company that sells Slim Fast and Axe, which are totally different brands. You have to make sure there's some continuity in your brand.

I: Why are stories important to business?

T: Stories are important to business because, when you come right down to it, that's what people are buying. They're buying the story behind your brand. Why else would someone pay four bucks for a cup of coffee at one place when they could buy a cup of coffee at another store for a dollar? For that matter, they could probably make it at home for a quarter. Why are they paying the extra three bucks? They're paying for the story. Maybe it makes them feel adventurous. Maybe it makes them forget the pile of paperwork sitting on their desk at home.

> *"Consumers are buying the story behind the brand. Prospects are sick of being sold to, so they put up barriers. Stories sneak past the barriers and create a connection."*

We see it with running shoes too. You could probably buy a very similar pair of running shoes as some of the expensive brands for about eight or ten bucks, but some people spend up to two hundred dollars on a pair of running shoes. Why? Because the brand says, "Just do it," or "Go for it."

Consumers are buying the story behind the brand. Seth Godin actually made that point about Puma running shoes. People are buying the inspiration—the feeling that if they wear these running shoes, they're invincible and can do anything.

The reason stories are so important in business is because prospects are sick of being sold to, so they put up barriers. Stories sneak past the barriers. We're all sick of being sold to, but if you tell a good story, it creates connection. People listen, they're entertained, prospects get interested, and they get involved. They sense intimacy and, thus, they don't feel defensive.

The other thing that is so great about stories is that they distinguish you from your competition. They make you easier to remember. When you go to a networking meeting, entrepreneurs stand up and list what's so great about them. Even TV commercials list benefits. People don't remember lists, but they will remember a good story that demonstrates your benefits.

I: What are some things to keep in mind when telling stories?

T: When you're telling a story, name the people: Joe, Sister Mary Catherine, etc. (By the way, when in doubt, throw some nuns into the story—people love stories with nuns.) Paint a picture in your stories. Use words like paintbrushes. Make us see it, make it colorful, and put yourself in the story. Create suspense and also use humor in your stories.

Tell the truth in your stories. You know how most cough syrup medicines taste pretty rotten? I don't know if you have this in the U.S., but in Canada we have a cough syrup called Buckley's Mixture. It has a great tagline: "It tastes awful. And it works." How brilliant is that? They were so honest with us by admitting that it tastes awful, so why would they lie to us about the rest? It must work, because they admitted their flaw, they admitted their vulnerability, and they also said that it works. Truth is a very effective marketing tool when you're telling stories.

During the election race between Barak Obama and John McCain, Obama used the technique of naming people, such as "Joe the plumber." In a recent State of the Union address, he picked particular people out of the audience and used them as examples. Instead of just preaching at us, he told individual stories. He named people and described where they work, and now they're more memorable to us, and he sounds less boring.

I: In your book, *Step Into the Spotlight,* you discuss the importance of having a thirty-second introduction or infomercial. Is it really possible to attract a new client in just thirty seconds?

T: Yes. Over the eight or nine years I've been in business, I've attracted almost half of my clients with just a thirty-second networking infomercial.

Business professionals are always saying, "It's about long-term relationships. You can't get a client in thirty seconds." You always hear that, but do you remember Roger Bannister? For years everyone said, "It's impossible to run a four-minute mile; you can't do it, your body will explode."

But in 1954, Roger Bannister did it. I think another three hundred people did it within the following year because they understood that it could be done.

Let me be your Roger Bannister: if you make your thirty-second infomercial or your thirty-second intro interesting, you can absolutely attract new clients. It's not a shopping list of information, it's not a list of features and benefits, it's a mini show. You've got to wow your audience. Give them a story and make them realize they're thirsty for what you're selling. If you do your job well, people will line up when you're done speaking just to know more.

I: You talk about having a distinct look, and you mentioned Johnny Cash earlier. Can you tell us more about that concept?

T: There are a lot of country singers out there, but he had a distinct look, a distinct persona. He had a low voice. He and his band all wore black. He had some silly little story about how that was the only thing they had that matched, which is a cute story, but it was probably because they wanted to look like tough guys.

Then he recorded an album. His record company thought he was crazy, but he recorded a live album at Folsom Prison with maximum security inmates. It was a huge hit—*At Folsom Prison*. Then they recorded another album, *At San Quentin*.

Everything he did was consistent with his persona, and that's what entrepreneurs need to do—develop a persona. It's all about doing things to create a distinct impression in the marketplace.

I: You suggest using humor, but what if you're not funny?

T: Humor is not just about telling jokes. Humor is a state of mind. It's about spontaneity, openness, honesty, recognition of universal truth, and common experience. There was a *Seinfeld* episode in which Jerry had reserved a rental car. He showed up to get it and it wasn't ready for him, and he says, "But I have a reservation!" They said, "Yes, but I'm sorry sir, we're out of those cars." He says, "Well isn't the whole point of a reservation that you *have* the car?"

In another episode he went to a Chinese restaurant and had to wait for half an hour; the whole episode is about waiting in the lobby. We laugh, not because he's telling funny jokes, but because we've all been there.

There was a movie in the 80s called *Punchline* with Sally Field and Tom Hanks. Sally played a housewife who paid five hundred dollars to buy some jokes for a comedy club, and she bombed. Tom Hanks's character tried to teach her the same thing I'm trying to teach entrepreneurs: it's not about standing there and telling silly little jokes, it's about telling your story and telling it in such an open, honest way that people recognize *their* story.

For example, I wrote a song called "Broccoli's On Sale at Dominion," which was about my Jewish mother. I had people of every nationality coming up to me —Filipinos, Norwegians, and even a Chinese bass player—saying, "That's my mother!"

When you create a persona and you use humor, it reaches beyond barriers and it resonates with people. You don't have to worry at all about being funny. You don't want to be goofy. You definitely don't want to be corny. But witty is always good.

I: Can you give an example of people, brands, or companies that are successfully using show business tactics?

T: I mentioned Mac and Apple, and Steve Jobs really understands the power of stories. There's also Emeril Lagasse. He was just a regular chef who used so much humor that the first time I saw him, I thought he was a comedian who was a guest on a cooking show. I didn't realize he was a chef who had a good sense of humor.

Emeril created his own lines, which is another great show business tactic. Emeril says, "Kick it up a notch," or "BAM!" Survivor uses, "voting someone off the island," and Donald Trump has, "You're fired!" Having a line you repeat is a great show business tactic.

A company in Canada, Roots, makes items like clothing and shoes. They understand the celebrity factor. They hang out with celebrities and get them to wear Roots brand clothing, and the celebrity factor rubs off on them. That's another show business tactic.

Kaile Warren understands the power of a good tagline. He was really struggling in the handyman business until he renamed his company Rent-A-Husband and came up with a great tagline: "Tall, dark, and handy." Once he started using that line, his business started to do really well. I think he even had a regular guest spot on a national TV show.

Wendy's used humor in their "Where's the beef?" commercials. Philip Morris does the same in the Marlboro Man commercials. Marlboro and Virginia Slims both know how to build brand personality. They're both cigarette brands—just tobacco in a case—but they have distinct brand personalities—distinct personas. There are tons and tons of great examples out there.

I: Why are professionals hesitant to include show business tactics?

T: They're scared they might look stupid. They secretly want to get noticed, but they're also afraid to be different; I find this especially true when it comes to independent professionals, coaches, and trainers. They're afraid of taking a risk.

You have to have thick skin to be a star. You might be out of fashion for a while. If you're an employee, there is a real risk in using some of these tactics. One of two things might happen: you might get fired, or you might get the corner office and a promotion.

There is a risk. There's a company called Big Ass Fans. They sell large fans that would be used in places like auditoriums. A lot of people hate their name. They find it very offensive. They get hate mail which they proudly post on their Web site. But for every piece of hate mail they get, they get tons of fan mail as well. When I studied them, they went from 7.4 million in revenue to 26.9 million in just three years. Why? Because they took a risk and they used show business tactics.

I: Can you share three tips our readers can put into action right away?

T: Absolutely!

Figure out what you're really selling. Altamira (later bought by National Bank) was brilliant when it came to this. They were a mutual funds company that wanted to convey the message that you've got to take care of your future. They ran a print ad showing an eighty-something-year-old, gray-haired granny wearing a Wal-Mart style smock like the ones greeters wear, and the copy underneath it said, "Is continuing to work part of your retirement plan?" Brilliant.

Another advertising campaign featured babies in tire swings "because a lot is riding on your tires." That company had figured out that they were selling safety and peace of mind. So figure out what you're really selling.

Identify your story and connect it to what you're selling. Dig deep and look for color. A client came to me to help her with a speech. It was kind of a dry, how-to speech to promote her speakers bureau. She wasn't a professional speaker herself, but she was speaking to a group of professional speakers, and she was somewhat scared.

When I interviewed her, I found out that she grew up on a tomato farm and that when she was eight years old, she helped her dad pick the tomatoes and take them to market.

I said, "Tomatoes are colorful, so why don't you use this analogy?" She did, and she said, "Some speakers are still too green. Some are still seedlings. Others are ripe, plump, juicy, and ready for market. And others are just plain rotten." For the first time in her life there was a line of people waiting to speak to her afterward.

Write a thirty-second spot—a mini show—to tell your story. It doesn't work well to use this thirty-second spot when you're one-on-one with someone because it doesn't feel real. I've seen people do it. Don't do it. If you're talking one-on-one with someone, just have a short tagline prepared. If you have an audience of twenty people, then have this mini show ready.

I: What's the most valuable piece of advice you can give anyone who's trying to make an impact?

T: This is something I learned as a litigation lawyer and as an actress in show business: You have to know when to sit down and shut up.

Chapter
9

If You Can Dream It,
You Can Do It
James Malinchak

Chapter 9
If You Can Dream It, You Can Do It
James Malinchak

James Malinchak has delivered over 2,200 motivational presentations at conferences and meetings worldwide, and was named Consummate Speaker of the Year by *Sharing Ideas* professional speakers' magazine. He has appeared in *USA Today, The Wall Street Journal,* and in several hundred other publications.

James began his sales career right out of college as a stockbroker with a major Wall Street investment firm and was awarded Most Outstanding Performance twice and Number One in New Account Openings twice. While in his twenties, James became a partner in a company that handled investments for many famous entertainers, authors, and professional athletes.

Currently, James owns three businesses, has authored eight books, and has read and researched over 1,500 books on personal and professional development. He is a contributing author and served as Associate Editor for the number one *New York Times* best-selling book series, *Chicken Soup for the Soul,* with his own personal stories published in *Chicken Soup for the Teenage Soul, Chicken Soup for the Kid's Soul,* and *Chicken Soup for the Prisoner's Soul.* James is also the co-author of the upcoming book, *Chicken Soup for the Athlete's Soul.* James mixes enthusiasm and humor with motivational stories to deliver a high-content message that empowers audiences to achieve extraordinary results.

I: James, what inspires you?

JM: It goes back to when I grew up in a small steel mill town. I actually conduct speaker trainings now and a lot of people have come to me and have said, "You've done so well as a highly paid motivational speaker, and I have a story (or a message or some experience), and I know things that I could teach other people, but how do you do this? You weren't famous. Nothing significant ever happened. You didn't win a Super Bowl, you didn't win a TV show contest, but you created this amazing speaking career. How did you do that? Give me some tips."

I always tell them, "The first thing you have to do when you meet anyone, or when you're giving a presentation anywhere, is you always have to tell a little bit about yourself and how you got started." A friend of mine, who is one of my long-time coaching members, taught me something years ago. He said, "No one will ever hear you until they know you."

What inspires me is telling others about where I got started, because when you hear that from others and you reflect on your own personal story of where you got started, I think that's what inspires most people. Sometimes you just have to pinch yourself and say, "Wow, I'm a blessed person!" Look at your life—whether it's your family or something significant you've done in business—and step back and remember where you started.

What inspires me most is continually remembering where I started. I always say, "I'm a very blessed person, and I'm just a steel mill town kid who happened to do some things right."

What I mean is that I grew up in a tiny steel mill town outside of Pittsburgh, Pennsylvania, with a population of about six thousand to maybe eight thousand people. We didn't have much growing up. Mom worked as a lunch mother at the school serving lunches to all the kids, and my dad worked in the steel mill for over thirty years.

We didn't have much, and growing up I never thought that I would be able to do some of the things I'm blessed to do today. It never crossed my mind. I had goals, but I never thought someone like me, living where I lived and coming from my background, could ever do things like this.

I had a mentor—an eighth grade teacher by the name of Mrs. Monaghan—who shared a quote by Walt Disney, and it always stuck with me: "If you can dream it, you can do it." I don't know why it stuck with me, but that has served as an inspiration.

This is what I relay to people now when I speak at corporations, associations, business conventions, community groups, colleges, universities, or youth organizations. Every time I speak, I always say, "It's not about where you *start* in life—it's about where you decide to *finish*."

One thing that keeps your fuel tank full is remembering where you started. If you are just starting out, and you would like to go to a higher place in your life right now, you've got to understand the quote from Walt Disney. You've got to intelligently lay out a plan for how to take the right steps to do what it is you want to do. It doesn't matter where you are, it matters where you decide to finish. I don't care where you are in your life right now, the question is, where do you want to be?

You also have to get rid of your excuses, because everyone has excuses. They're pretty good excuses, and every excuse you give yourself will always be right: "Oh yeah, I'd like to have a great marriage, *but* . . . " or "I'd like to be the first person in my family to go to college and get a degree, *but* . . . " or "I'd like to leave my job working for someone else and start my own business, *but* . . . " or "I'd like to be a millionaire, *but* . . . " or "I'd like to achieve this goal, *but* . . . " or "I'd like to achieve that dream, *but...* "

The only thing that stops you from going from where you are to where you want to be is a big "but," so you have to get your "but" out of the way!

I'm very blessed to have been on ABC's reality TV show *Secret Millionaire*. If someone had told me five years ago that I would end up on ABC primetime television because of what I've done as a speaker, because of what I've accomplished by teaching others how to monetize their mission—their story, their message—to become highly paid speakers telling their own stories, I would have asked what they were smoking, because five years ago I had that "but" still in my head.

Even though I had been blessed to achieve certain things, I still had that "but" when it came to something big like primetime television. Why would they choose me? I'm just a steel mill town kid. You have to get your "but" out of the way, because, "If you can dream it, you can do it."

I: How do you inspire others?

JM: I think we all inspire other people through our stories of what we've overcome in our lives. One of the things I've studied for years is Hollywood movies. Watch the psychology behind Hollywood movies—what movies we always like and that always appeal to and attract the public. They're the movies where someone overcomes something.

Think about some of the most inspirational movies of all time—such as *Rocky*—about an underdog. We root for the underdog. Why? Because we want to see him prevail. We want to see Rocky win and to come through the struggle.

Look at a football movie like *Rudy* about a guy going to Notre Dame to play football. Rudy is a good friend of mine—the real Rudy, not the actor. Why did we like *Rudy*? Because it was about an underdog. The character was going through a struggle, pain.

Look at a hockey movie such as *Miracle* about the United States hockey team defeating the Russian hockey team in the Olympics. Why did that appeal to us? Because they weren't supposed to win. They were beaten up; there was no way they could beat the Russian hockey team.

Look at a horse movie like *Seabiscuit*. Look at another boxing movie like *Cinderella Man* or *The Fighter*. What you quickly learn is that the reason those movies inspire us is because we *are* those movies. We have a story like that within us, no matter what it is: a story of struggle, a story of pain, a story of triumph, a story of finding the love of our life after so much struggling. We have stories in our lives of families coming back together after not talking to each other for years and finally overcoming that adversity.

"What inspires me is the story of struggle, triumph, overcoming adversity, not quitting, and never giving up. We are those people. We all share that story."

What inspires me, and what I think inspires everyone, is the story of struggle, triumph, overcoming adversity, not quitting, and never giving up—the story of Rocky getting knocked down and standing up again and again and again. We *are* those people. We all share that story. It inspires me, and I think what inspires everyone is their own story.

I'm not saying your story has to be something like winning the heavyweight boxing championship of the world like in *Rocky*, but your story might be, "I worked three jobs as a single parent and I busted my butt, and because of that I have great kids." That is an amazingly inspirational story, and it inspires other people. Someone can look at you and say, "If you did it and you didn't quit, then maybe I can do it too." You give them hope. What inspires me are the stories of people who just won't quit no matter how tough it seems and no matter what the circumstances are.

I: I agree, because if you watch reality shows like *The Biggest Loser*—most of us have struggled with weight at some point—you see people overcoming huge challenges and you find yourself rooting for them; you really want them to make it. This mind-set is permeating our culture in a lot of different ways

JM: Yes, it's the process of someone coming from where they were and seeing the transformation and the beautiful change they made in their lives—it doesn't even have to be specifically a weight-loss-focused show. If you look at the underlying message, it's about seeing someone come through something tough and not quit—it's going from mess to success.

That's what *Secret Millionaire* is all about. That's why it's changing the lives of millions of people all over the world. I basically lived in a ghetto on less than forty-five dollars for a whole week. That was all the money I had to live on.

The whole premise of the show is very inspirational. I take millionaires out of their everyday lifestyle and put them into situations they're not used to being in to find out if they can survive. There I was, taken out of my lifestyle in Las Vegas, and thrust into a tough economic area where I was basically living in a ghetto. I was living in a very small apartment on $44.62 for an entire week.

I was volunteering in the community, looking for amazing, beautiful, spirited people who were serving others. No one knew who I was. The camera crew that was with me from ABC was staged as if they were shooting a documentary on volunteer groups. No one knew we were filming a reality TV show. They didn't want anyone to act out of the ordinary; they just wanted them to be themselves.

I was sweeping streets, cleaning up trash, helping young kids with their homework in afterschool programs—the same things these volunteers were doing to get kids off the streets. I was watching these amazing spirits who were doing this for no other reason than to give back, to support others, and to lift up someone else.

At the end of the week, I revealed my identity, and I shared with everyone that I was not actually a struggling poor person—that in fact I am actually a millionaire. And then I opened up my checkbook and told them, "I have been so inspired by what you're doing and the amazing spirit you show that I'd like to give you this check for . . . " Then I started writing checks for $50,000, $20,000, $10,000, or for whatever it was. I gave them some financial resources so they could continue to carry out their mission of serving and loving.

I gave away over $100,000, but it wasn't about the money. The money certainly helped; if you've got an electric bill coming due and you don't have the money in your bank account, you can try and deposit with the credit collecting company all the hope, inspiration, intention, and Law of Attraction stuff you want, but if you don't have the money in your bank account, you can't pay the bill.

The money definitely helped those folks, no doubt about it. It kept some people from losing their homes and it got some of the people out of the process of having to close their business. The money helped, but here's what I quickly noticed: They received much more than the money. They received a deeper spiritual gift—hope.

The awarding of the check—the money—symbolized that someone recognized them and the great stuff they were doing. It said, "You can't quit doing what you're doing." Sure, the money helped to pay their bills, but what I really did, I believe, was I gave them hope, and that's priceless. When someone's at the end of their rope, they need hope.

I: Yes they do. That's fabulous. Why did you choose this arena for your life's great work?

JM: I didn't, it actually chose me. I was a stockbroker—a financial consultant—managing people's money. I had clients who were entertainers and professional athletes and celebrities. I was watching the stock market and managing their investments.

I won some awards in my company. During my first year there I won Most Outstanding Performance twice and Number One in Account Openings twice. There were people who were fifteen or twenty years into the business who were not doing that. Because I won those awards at such a young age and within such a short amount of time, I was asked to speak and training others within the company on how I did it.

So I started speaking and training, and I did a training presentation in New York City. I think it was in the World Trade Center, actually. Someone there saw me speak, called his father back in Southern California and said, "We just had this guy speak, and he was very uplifting and motivational, but he gave really good content also. It was stuff we could use. You might want to consider having him come and speak to your employees."

I get a call, and this guy says, "My son heard you speak, and I want to see about having you come and speak to our employees."

I asked, "What do you want me to speak about? I'm not a speaker, I just happened to do this training because they asked me to do it."

He said, "I just want you to talk about your story and how you stayed motivated and inspired to keep doing great work and doing great things."

I asked, "How long do you want me to speak for?"

He said, "I need you to speak for about an hour."

I was thinking that would be pretty simple. I had just done a training that lasted about three hours and I was just teaching what I knew. If I could do three hours, I could fill one hour. Then he asked me another question. He asked, "How much do you charge?"

I had no clue. That was so foreign to me. I thought, *They're going to pay me to do this?*

I've learned one thing in business: when someone asks you a question and you are dumbfounded and baffled and you don't know the answer, there are a couple of lines that you can say to throw the question back to them so that they have to answer it.

So he asked, "How much do you charge?"
I said, "How much you got?"

He said, "Well, we paid the last guy about five thousand bucks."

I almost fell off my chair. I asked, "How long do you want me to talk again?"

He said, "Could you speak for about an hour? Would you do that for us?"

I'm thinking, *For five thousand bucks I'll not only speak for the hour, I'll wash your car, I'll go get your dry cleaning . . .*

Like I said, it sort of picked me, because I never knew anything about how to get started in speaking. I had no clue whatsoever. Then suddenly here's this man talking about hiring me for one hour to speak, offering to pay me $5,000, and acting like it was something he does all the time.

I: I hope you accepted.

JM: I had to get my tongue out of my throat—I was swallowing it. I couldn't believe it. Are you kidding me? For an hour? After I got off the ground from where I fell off my chair, I took a gulp and said, "I think that will work."

I went and gave a motivational talk. They loved it. They gave me a check for five thousand dollars for an hour. I thought, *You've got to be kidding me!*

Then they said, "Would you be willing to speak at two more of our offices? Would you be willing to accept the same fee?"

Again I thought, *You've got to be kidding me!* I did three talks, made fifteen thousand dollars for three hours of work, and I said, "Wait a minute—I'm on to something here!" That's when I realized there are two sides to professional speaking. There's your message and what you deliver, and then there is the business side, and it is a huge business. It's a billion dollar industry with conventions and colleges and corporations. I thought, *Wait a minute, if they're going to pay me to help people and inspire people and do something I love to do, I'm going to figure out how to make this work.*

I did, and I've done so many presentations and helped so many people, but I got compensated for it too. I could have been doing it for free, but I realized it was a business.

To answer your question, it picked me, I didn't pick it. I didn't even know it existed. I compare it to being an entertainer who loves to sing and who all of a sudden is getting *paid* to sing, getting paid to record an album, or getting paid to put on a concert. I feel like I've never worked a day in my life because I'm getting paid to do something I love to do which is to speak and help people.

I: How do you define success?

JM: It's simple. I defined success years ago. It's happiness with myself, happiness with my life, happiness doing what I want to do when I want to do it and however I want to do it.

I read an article years ago in which Mother Teresa said that one of her great pleasures in life was holding the hands of people as they were "transitioning"—as they were dying. Society tells us that success equals money, and that could be true to a certain extent, but Mother Teresa held people's hands when they were dying and found great joy in that.

Does that mean she's not successful because maybe she wasn't wealthy? I think she was extremely successful. If you are a parent and you have the great pleasure of raising amazing kids and getting to spend time with your spouse or whatever that looks like for you and you're happy, isn't that success?

Society equates success with money and material things and programs us to think that way too. I'm not saying that can't be part of success; it's definitely part of success in business, because if a business is not making money and profiting, then it is not really successful. But to me, success is all about happiness—it's about doing what I want, when I want, wherever I want, with whomever I want, however much I want.

That's how I've always defined success. The minute I'm not happy doing something in my life, I don't feel like I'm successful, and I change it. I have a rule for my business: I absolutely will not work with anyone who irritates me. Let me tell you why.

I lost my sister, Vicki, years ago to a brain tumor. She died very unexpectedly. She was okay, and then three months later she collapsed and died. It taught me that life is too short to be around people who irritate you, who bring you down, who you don't want to be around, and who you don't like being around. Why would you want to be around them?

I have 160 coaching members I consult and coach for. The fees to coach with me are $20,000 a year, $60,000 a year, and $100,000 a year. I have 160 members in my coaching and consulting group. I got a text message recently that one of my dear clients unexpectedly had a massive heart attack and died. It reminded me that life is too short to spend your time around people you don't like being around. Do what you like to do and be with the people you want to be with.

Every now and then life reminds us that we have to do a happiness check and make sure we're only around people we like to be around, that we're happy, and that we're only doing things we like to do.

"I'm not saying money is not important, but a lot of people I see in business pursue only money and they forget about everything else. You've got to have a balance of all mechanisms. If all you pursue is wealth and you lose your health, are you really successful?"

I: I think that's true, and who you surround yourself with does determine your attitude. I say success is "user-defined." Each person has to determine his or her own meaning of success. Like you said, society says it's about how much money you make or rising through the ranks in business, but that's not necessarily the case for everyone. You might rise through the ranks of business, but your real love and passion might be for something totally different.

JM: If all you pursue is wealth and you lose your health, are you really successful? Think about that. I'm not saying money is not important; if you don't have money, you can't eat. It's that simple. If your church needs a roof put on or if you have six hungry kids in a city and there is no food, you can do all the wishing and hoping you can, but the bottom line is you need money to provide for basic needs.

I'm not saying money is not important, but a lot of people I see in business pursue *only* money and they forget about everything else. They forget about their family. They're not balanced. They forget about their lifestyle and doing the things they love to do. They forget about their health, and their health declines because of it.

You've got to have a balance of all mechanisms. The bottom line is, when we die, we are not taking anything we have here with us. We're all going out the same way we came in, and that's with nothing.

I: What is the most powerful moment of success or life-changing experience for you?

JM: I got a telephone call one day—this was several years ago—from my dad. He said my sister Vicki had collapsed and was in the hospital with the right side of her body paralyzed.

This was shocking for me because I was with Vicki two weeks before this happened and she was perfectly fine. As a matter of fact, I'll tell you what we did. We went to the movies, we went to the mall, we ate some pizza, and then we were just hanging out as brother and sister.

Initially we thought it had to be a pinched nerve in Vicki's back, because Vicki was a young person. She was thirty-eight years old. The first set of test results came back—it wasn't a pinched nerve. Then we thought maybe Vicki had a stroke because medical research is now telling us that young people can have strokes. The second set of results came back— it wasn't a stroke.

A few days went by, and I could not get Vicki on the phone. Finally, I was connected to her new room. Vicki answered the phone, and I got all excited, and I said, "Hey, Vicki! How are you?"

She asked, "Did you hear?"

I got even more excited. I said, "What? Did they figure it out? Everything is okay? You're coming home? Is that why you're in a new room, because they upgraded you and everything's fine and you're coming home?"

She said, "No. I have a brain tumor, and the doctors say I'm going to die in three months."

I didn't know what to say. I just remember thinking, *This doesn't happen to my sister*. We never think these kinds of things will happen to people we love. This stuff happens to other people's brothers, sisters, grandmas, grandpas, moms, dads, and friends.

I hope no one ever experiences what I'm about to say I experienced when she said those words to me. I certainly hope I don't ever experience it again, because it was the scariest thing I have ever experienced in my entire life.

When she said that to me, I tried to speak, but nothing came out of my mouth. You hear people say they tried talking and nothing came out, and you figure they just decided not to talk. No. I am telling you I was talking to Vicki but not a single sound was coming out of my mouth. To this day I don't know how that happened; I know I was talking. I don't know if my body was in shock or what, but I was talking, and there was nothing coming out of my mouth.

Sadly, three and a half months later Vicki passed away. It taught me a very valuable lesson about life: life is short. Life is too short to not do what you want, when you want, where you want, and with whomever you want.

That was a life-changing moment for me. You only get one shot at this life—you might as well enjoy it and live it to the fullest. And when I say live it to the fullest, I mean live it the way *you* want to live it. If you're not happy being in a relationship with someone, get out of it. Why would you want to go through agony?

I don't make many guarantees, especially when I speak for groups. But I'm going to guarantee you one thing that I know as sure as I'm breathing, and that is this: Not a single one of us is guaranteed tomorrow. Not one of us. So why would you want to live your life being unhappy?"

That, to me, was the inspirational turning point. I have to tell you, I never thought, in my entire life, that anything would come close to the experience I had with Vicki—that brother and sister time we spent together before she passed away and the things I learned from that experience. I never thought anything in my life would ever come close.

But being on *Secret Millionaire*—going through the journey and seeing the amazing people and how it changed my life more than the money changed their lives—is second. In my heart, it's not as life-changing as being with my sister, because that's always going to be special because she was my sister. But *Secret Millionaire,* the people I met, and what the producers and the people on the show allowed me to experience was one of the greatest things I've ever done.

I: When you're changing that many lives, definitely.

JM: Here's what's important though—they changed my life more than my money changed theirs.

I: What are the three most important personal tips you could share for achievement and fulfillment?

JM: First, I want to say that you can be, do, and have anything you desire in life. It may be difficult and it may seem unfathomable, but someone, somewhere has already blazed the trail, so figure out who that person is and learn from them. I don't care what you have to invest to learn from them. But notice I didn't say *spend money*.

All the information for anything you want to do in life is already out there. There are books, CDs, seminars, consulting programs, coaching programs, etc. If you want to learn how to make money in real estate, there are people who have already done it and can teach you how to do it. If you want to learn how to get in shape, there are trainers and books—more books than you could imagine. If you want to have a great marriage, there are people out there who have great marriages. If you want to be a great parent, there are people who have great parenting skills. Go talk with them. Go learn from them.

> *"You can be, do, and have anything you desire in life. It may be difficult and it may seem unfathomable, but someone, somewhere has already blazed the trail, so figure out who that person is and learn from them."*

All the information for anything you want to do in any area of your life is out there, but you have to get off your assets and go get it. You have to do something about it.

Three Secrets to Success

1. Mind-Set
This is all about how you think. Rich people think differently than poor people. Healthy people think differently than unhealthy people. Those in shape think differently than those out of shape. Those who succeed in business think differently than those who don't succeed in business. It all comes down to your mind-set.

2. Skill Set
You can't just think about it and hope for it, you've got to actually

learn some specific skills that will help you achieve what it is you want to do.

Take speaking for example. A lot of people say, "I want to be a speaker. I have a message, and I want to empower people and inspire people. I'm a positive person!" That's great, that's your mind-set, but it takes a heck of a lot more than that. You have to combine it with a skill set.

You have to know what I call **The Five Ps**:
- **Positioning:** What's the right positioning for you as to who you are and what your message is?
- **Packaging:** What's the right packaging?
- **Presentation:** What's the right presentation, and how should it be structured to make an impact on the audience so that they love you and want to bring you back again and again?
- **Promotion:** What's the right promotion to get yourself and your story out? If no one knows about you, you're not going to make any money. You're going to sit at home rather than speaking.
- **Payment:** How do you get paid? What are the seven, eight, nine different ways you get paid as a speaker?

You have to learn how to tell stories from the stage. You have know who the people are who control the budgets and how to get them to choose you. That's a valuable skill set.

3. Get Off Your Assets
You've got to take action. Tony Robbins, who's a great positive influence for many people, says, "You have to take massive action." James Malinchak says, "You have to get off your assets and do something."

There are your three tips for achievement—*mindset, skill set,* and *get off your assets!*

Chapter 10

Propelling Your Productivity and Your Bottom Line
Dr. Sharon Melnick

Chapter 10
Propelling Your Productivity and Your Bottom Line
Dr. Sharon Melnick

Dr. Sharon Melnick is a coach and psychologist who helps talented and successful people get out of their own way. She parlayed ten years of psychology research at Harvard Medical School into a coaching practice that helps clients discover both why they have been approaching their life in a way that limits potential and how they can quickly build a new effectiveness that accelerates success.

Her coaching practice is divided between executive coaching, which is helping emerging leaders become successful senior executives, and business coaching, which is helping business owners develop the confidence to make money. She is also a leading authority in teaching busy professionals techniques to manage themselves instead of managing time, so they can be highly productive despite the stresses of the new economic climate. Sharon teaches clients her copyrighted Direct Path process, which shows how to go directly to the result they want and how to have an effective relationship with themselves without wasting effort on managing others' perceptions and things they can't control. Clients develop what she calls the "emotional intelligence" needed for financial independence.

Dr. Melnick serves as an expert for the American Management Association, the National Association of Women Executives, Success Television, and organizations such as Oracle Corp., Deutsche Bank, Visiting Nurses Service, Northwest Mutual, IBM, Pitney Bowes, and many others.

I: How did you start determining how people get in their own way and turn your career as a research psychologist at Harvard Medical School into a coaching business?

SM: The best way I could learn about the subject matter of how people get in their own way was by studying myself. I have lots of experience getting in my own way! While I was doing research at the medical school and starting a coaching practice, I was helping other people grow their businesses. I was helping employees rise through the ranks of leadership; yet inside, I was still doing things that were causing me to get in my own way.

I would have an idea about something I wanted to write or do, and I would sit on it for days, weeks, or sometimes even months before I would get it out the door. I was allowing other people to steal my time. I worried too much about what other people thought about me and was reactive to them. I spun my wheels and went in all kinds of directions trying to be all things to all people because I didn't own my own value. That, I think, is the basis of how people get in their own way.

I often tell about a time when I was invited to share my research at the White House and I declined the invitation. How about that for qualifying as someone who was getting in her own way? Again, it was because I didn't think I had anything of value to bring to them. I observed this in myself and also saw it happening for lots of other people.

In terms of how I made the transition from research, the research I was doing was based on intergenerational issues—what you bring with you from your own childhood into your parenting.

I conducted research to understand the process, and I developed methods to help parents coming from difficult childhoods avoid repeating the mistakes of their own parents, thus breaking that cycle. I was working with parents from all walks of life. Particularly the ones involved in business would say to me at a certain point in the process, "You know, I don't just do these things with my kids. I do this with my clients, my business partners, my boss, and my direct reports—with everyone in my life."

It helped me to appreciate the fact that what I was working on with them wasn't about parenting at all. It's about what you bring with you; the way you deal with yourself and with other people forms the foundation for everything you do in your life.

It was right about that time, ten or fifteen years ago, when the idea of corporate coaching and business coaching was coming into consciousness, and a lot of people were saying to me, "This is really what you do." I got trained on coaching techniques and then started talking about more things with people as it related to their career and fulfilling their potential rather than about their parenting; it has taken off since then.

I: What does the phrase *get out of your own way* or *you are your own worst enemy* mean to you?

SM: What I mean is that we all have an intention—a dream for our lives. What do you want or think you want? Do you act in service of it? Or do you do things that end up causing your own suffering?

"When we're growing up, we come to see ourselves through the eyes of other people. We need a certain amount of 'emotional oxygen.' Physical oxygen is what we need to breathe; emotional oxygen is what we need in order to feel worthy and valuable as human beings."

It's as though you're working really hard and cycling at seventy miles an hour, but you're cycling into a ninety-mile-an-hour headwind. I think we've all had that experience. If you boil it down, it's about trusting yourself, owning your own value, believing in yourself—however you want to describe it.

One of the things I carried with me from my research is that when we're growing up, we come to see ourselves through the eyes of other people. That's how we come to know who we are and what our worth is. We need a certain amount of "emotional oxygen." Physical oxygen is what we need to breathe; emotional oxygen is what we need in order to feel worthy and valuable as human beings.

As they are growing up, the people who become successful are those who are able to make that transition from getting that core experience of themselves from other people to getting it from within and from the reward they get from their own contribution. When you're not able to get that emotional oxygen from things you do on your own, it sets you up to act in ways that will make you "others" directed. That's what I mean when I say people are getting in their own way or that they are their own worst enemy. We're saying that so much energy and time goes into managing other people and trying to get what is needed from *them* instead of directly moving one's own life forward.

I: As psychologist by trade, what is your philosophy about coaching?

SM: What I do is really more about helping a person to self-manage or deal with themselves so that they can become the person they need to be.

Each of us is the instrument of our own success. As coaches, we talk to people about their goals, the results they want, and their behaviors. That's how results get actualized.

I am more likely to start off by asking a person who they want to be. I ask them to look out at that horizon point for their life and ask themselves, "What are the qualities and attributes present there?" My mission is to help them to become that person—to adopt that way of thinking, that way of feeling, and that way of behaving—so that they can move forward and coach themselves.

I can't control the results. I can't control whether they're going to take action. I can only help them to build that relationship with themselves so that they can get themselves to take action in the moment.

I do best practices coaching, helping people get their results, but I take it out of the "me versus the client" concept. It is more about helping them become the person *they* want to be. I find that once a person is consistently thinking, feeling, and acting like that person, they naturally continue to take those actions. It's not a matter of me being an accountability coach and asking what they are doing each week. They naturally step into it themselves.

I: Why is it that so many of us know what we should be doing to grow our business, yet we're not really doing it?

SM: We know what we should be doing. Many of us start off each day with a well-intentioned to-do list. We say, "This is what successful coaches are doing, and these are the actions I'm going to take." But we end the day asking ourselves, "Where did the day go?"

It's not so much about scheduling the actions or putting the actions down on paper; it's really about how you form that relationship with yourself and whether you're able to get *yourself* to do those things in the moment. There are so many things we do to get in our own way when it comes to our own productivity.

I: What is the one thing that distinguishes someone who will be successful from someone who won't be? What specific action does it take to become the successful individual?

SM: You have to be motivated and you have to have clarity about what the most important actions are. What is the best leveraged use of your time?

As business owners, we have to wear all of the different hats, so of course it is easy to get overwhelmed. There are very helpful time-management techniques we can learn though. Some of these include learning how to organize your stuff, how to schedule your time, and how to block your time. For example, if you have an e-mail marketing campaign you're going to be putting out, you can schedule a block of time into your calendar from 2:00 to 4:00 in afternoon. However, when 2:00 rolls around, it's not whether you've scheduled it into your calendar that's going to determine whether you actually do it. It has more to do with how you deal with yourself—whether you have a productively mind-set.

It depends on whether you know how to deal with other people in your life to create undistracted times and whether you know how to be proactive in letting them know that you need that time. If they come to you with an urgent request, you have to identify a way you can respectfully communicate that you'll be able to talk to them another time.

It's about whether you believe in the moment that what you have to say is important and valuable, because if you don't believe that at a deeper level, the time can come for you to write it up, but you're not going to be willing to hit the Send button.

It's about whether you can stay motivated and not be overly disappointed if you've sent out campaigns but haven't had the kind of response you were hoping for.

It's about whether you can organize yourself clearly in the moment and take all of things you are excited to say and boil them down to the one big idea that's going to be a hook for people.
These productivity tools and time-management techniques are very important. The structures will help you take action, but you also

have to have a productivity mind-set. You have to have the ability to deal with yourself. The equation for your success is time-management techniques or productivity tools *plus* a productivity mind-set.

I: What is a productivity mind-set?

SM: It's thinking about the result you want for your life and being able to focus on that. It's being able to deal with yourself and with other people so that no matter what is going on, you consistently take action toward the things that will move your life forward. The mind-set includes all of the ways you talk to yourself, the belief you have in yourself, and your ability look at situations differently and to change your perspective and your emotional state. It is all a part of the self-management tool kit.

I: What are some ways people get in the way of their own productivity?

SM: I'm actually coming out with an information product having to do with this, and there are four modules I'll review for you briefly.

Four Ways We Get in the Way of Our Own Productivity

1. Allowing Others to Interrupt and Distract Us
When it comes to this type of distraction, we typically think it is the other person who is doing the distracting, whether it's an assistant, a difficult client, a family member, or whoever it might be. The belief is that the other person needs to stop the disruptive behavior.

To look at it in this way is to give away your power. It is not taking responsibility for your own half in the situation; it's not controlling what you can control. Changing that perspective is one of the absolute foundations people need in order to get out of their own way in any situation.

There are many things we can do in these situations, even if others are knocking on the door or calling at unexpected times. For example, set up voice mail or an e-mail responder. Let people know when you need uninterrupted time. Another tip is to create a Frequently Asked Questions section on your Web site in order to minimize the number of people who are interrupting you for things you don't need to be spending your time on. This way you can spend your time on the inside work: owning your value and believing in the value of your time so that you and others will respect your time. Know what you will say in advance so that you can convincingly communicate with people who are infringing on your time.

It's really a mind-set. If you own the value of your own time, you will consider how you can use your time to get your message out and help people rather than letting other people steal it from you.

2. Experiencing Confidence-Related Issues

I've had students in my program who spent time following up with low-revenue clients or clients who may not have been as likely to come and work with them. Why would they do that? Because when they talk to those people, they feel good. They say, "We had a good conversation. I felt great. I didn't get the sale at the rate I think I deserve, but they told me they appreciated my time." Of course that's generous and that's good, but you can see how a person might be spending valuable time on low-level prospects just to feel good; it doesn't advance their business.

This also shows when people feel like they have to respond immediately to every e-mail. I definitely encourage high-quality service, but is that the best use of your time, or are you doing it just because you're trying to show people that you're perfect and always on? What's the best use of your time?

There are so many ways we get in our own way. When you don't own your own value—when you don't truly believe in yourself—all of these things are going to show up. You're going to allow your time, your energy, and your attention to be siphoned away by other people, and you're not going to be putting your time, energy, and attention into the things that are going to allow you to deliver on your gifts in a way that will be of highest service to you and to other people.

3. Lacking a Sense of Clarity

So many of us are trying to grow our businesses, and there are so many different marketing approaches—it's the proverbial shiny new penny. The most successful individuals have a clear idea of the value they bring, a very clear message, and most importantly they have a clear business model and they spend their time only on efforts that are helping to grow that business. They don't just say, "I want to make X amount of money and however it comes in is great, so let me spread myself thin all over the place."

When you're getting in your own way, often it's because you're spending your time, energy, and attention trying to manage other people—particularly their perceptions of you. You're not owning your value at a deeper level.

4. "Going Indirect"

Again, this has to do with your attention going to other people and trying to manage them, trying to get your emotional oxygen from other people, and trying to hear from other people in order to own your value.

> *"When you're getting in your own way, often it's because you're spending your time, energy, and attention trying to manage other people—particularly their perceptions of you. You're not owning your value at a deeper level."*

"Going direct" is not worrying about whether you're enough or about what people think of you, but about considering the contribution you were put here to make. What is the specific skill set you bring to your work? What are the specific experiences and the specific transformations you are uniquely qualified to present to your clients?

Focus on the end user of your work and on how you can help your clients make that transformation. This will allow you to focus your time, energy, and attention on building your business and getting a clear message across. Don't focus on what other people are thinking about you. Focus on providing effective transformation for your clients. In doing this, you'll see the appreciation come back to you, helping you to grow and to own your value.

When considering what your fees should be, don't just sit there at your desk and ask, "Am I enough? Am I worth it? What do other people think I'm worth?" Get out of your own head about it! Just take action and let the market help you determine your value. Don't give in to behaviors that only provide short-term appreciation. I call it a sugar high when someone says, "I think you're a great person," or "I appreciate you doing that." Don't necessarily put all of your efforts into receiving that kind of feedback. Put your efforts into bringing your gifts to the world. That will allow you to reap a much larger reward.

I: What about procrastination and the fear of failure?

SM: Would you be hopeless if you went for it and it didn't work out?

It's about trying to hold on to hope. As long as you don't go for it, you can say to yourself, "I just have to develop more confidence," or "Someday I'm going to be really successful in my business." You get to live with yourself by thinking, *I could still be that person* rather than going for it, because if you go for it and it doesn't work out, you risk losing all hope.

All you have to do is to be able to tell yourself a different story and select a different mantra, such as, "Whoever makes the most mistakes wins." If you haven't dealt with yourself like that in the past, then you're holding on to hope and procrastinating.

I: What do beliefs have to do with how we get in our own way?

SM: At the root of how we get in our own way is a deep conviction that we're, not enough, not deserving, or whatever variation it is for you. In my work—or at least during the first part of the process of helping someone get out of their own way—I help people make the connection between the beliefs they have about themselves and how those beliefs set them up to act.

In many of the things I have mentioned, you can hear the beliefs that are getting in the way: "It is up to other people to change their behavior if they're interrupting me," or "My ideas aren't important," or "People aren't going to be persuaded by me, so that's why I'm not going to send out my work." I believe that beliefs are the foundation, and the techniques I teach help people to change their beliefs quickly.

It's not only about choosing to change one's beliefs; it has to come from experience. That's why the whole idea of "going direct" is about putting your efforts into actions that will not necessarily get you immediate feedback and help you feel differently about yourself now, but will instead lead to lasting accomplishments in the long run. No one can take away those accomplishments. They lead to a different experience of yourself, and that's one of the most powerful and enduring ways to change your beliefs.

Chapter 11

Your Story Is Your Success
Lisa Bloom

Chapter 11
Your Story Is Your Success
Lisa Bloom

Lisa Bloom grew up in a traditional home in Ireland, surrounded by beautiful countryside, whimsical tales of pixies and leprechauns, and the warmth of Jewish practice. As a child, she loved to hear and tell stories. Lisa has traveled widely and taken on many jobs, including stable girl, galley slave, bartender, photographer, rape crisis counselor, HR manager, coach, mother, writer, entrepreneur, trainer, and storyteller. She is convinced that telling a good story is the remedy for most ills. Lisa earned a BA from Tel Aviv University and an MBA from Boston University.

Lisa is the founder of Story Coach, Inc., developing creative solutions for coaches, trainers, and entrepreneurs to beat exhaustion, overwhelm, and stress. Lisa helps her clients find confidence and balance as they build their business by finding their success story. Lisa's certified Story Coach Training Program, which is ICF accredited, is one of a kind worldwide and trains coaches in the powerful use of storytelling in coaching. She lives in Israel with her partner and their four boys.

I: How did you get started? What drew you into storytelling and coaching?

LB: Originally I was working in development and training in large organizations. I loved the classroom training, and I found that the more I used stories as I trained, the more engaging my trainings were.

My classes became more interesting and people were asking more questions. In a sense, I was meeting my personal goals and the organizational goals by engaging people and helping them to learn better and to be more motivated. Not only were they more motivated, but they were also implementing what they were learning at a higher level, so their productivity was rising.

I saw how it affected my goals as a trainer and as a training manager, and I suddenly understood the power of storytelling. At first I would do it spontaneously; I would make up stories as I went along because that's something I have always done. I've been telling stories my whole life, so when a friend said to me, "You should coach—that's what you do," it made sense that I would coach in the same way I told stories.

When I started realizing how effective stories are and how they can be applied to coaching, it was a breakthrough for me in terms of how I approached my coaching practice and the specific niche I wanted to pursue.

I: Could you give an example? Would you mind telling a story?

LB: I'd love to. There's nothing I love more, actually. I'm going to tell you a story that I used at the start of the storytelling program I'm involved in at the moment.

The Picture of Peace (Author Unknown)

There was once a king who offered a prize to the artist who could paint the best picture of peace. He sent out a notice to the whole kingdom that whoever could create the most perfect picture of peace would be given a great prize. Many artists tried—in fact, many people who weren't even artists tried—and many, many pictures were sent to the palace. The king looked at all of them. He spent quite some time—days in fact. Finally, after so much deliberation, he was down to the final two and he had to choose between them.

The first picture showed a calm lake, and the lake was a perfect mirror for the peaceful mansions that towered around it. Over the mansions were fluffy white clouds floating in a perfect blue sky, and everyone who saw this picture said it was the perfect picture of peace.

The second picture also depicted mansions, but these mansions were bare and rugged, and above them was an angry gray sky where rain and lightning flashed. Down the side of one mansion there tumbled a waterfall that was foaming, and it didn't appear to be a peaceful place at all. But when the king looked closely, he saw that behind the waterfall there was a tiny bush growing on a rock, and inside the bush, a mother bird had built her nest. There, in the midst of the rush of angry water, the mother bird sat on her nest, and she was the perfect picture of peace.

In the end, the king chose the second picture because, as he explained, peace is not only found in places where there is no noise or trouble or hard work; peace is found in the midst of things as they are. When there's calm in your heart, that is real peace.

"When you tell a story, people are drawn into the space and the beauty of the story. The place where stories are held within us receives the message in a very different way."

I: That is quite a descriptive story! How would you use a story like this?

LB: There are many uses for storytelling in coaching, but one of the ways—what I've just given an example of—is to use stories as illustrations. Stories draw people closer to issues that may be hard to broach or difficult for them to get a handle on. Stories can also be used simply to offer a sense of hope or to motivate.

This particular story is a beautiful, descriptive, calm, and powerful way to give a person a sense of the inner peace they might be missing in themselves. It can help them understand that peace isn't about everything being perfect and calm, but that peace is present even when things seem difficult and out of reach.

You can say that to a person directly, and it may have an effect or it may not, but when you tell a story, people are drawn into the space and the beauty of the story. The place where stories are held within us receives the message in a very different way. The story takes on a life of its own and it does the work for you. It's an incredibly powerful way to send a message or to create this illustrative process where people can get closer to issues that in other circumstances they may not even be able to consider.

I: What are some other ways stories can be used?
LB: Stories can be used in so many ways, but one way is as a

marketing technique. Understanding our own story and creating the story of ourselves is a great way to market ourselves. So many successful people and successful companies have a compelling story behind them, and generally speaking, it's the story that we remember.

I believe that everyone has a compelling story; everyone has interesting life events that have led them to the very place where they are right now in their lives. When we connect with that powerful story—when we create the story and use it effectively—it becomes a very powerful marketing technique. In a sense, it's a business tool.

I: So if the agenda is all about the client, how do you bring in storytelling?

LB: That's a question coaches ask me a lot. They say, "Hang on a second. We're not supposed to talk so much. We're supposed to listen and ask questions. How can we spend so much time telling stories?"

Telling a story in the way that I demonstrated, in this illustrative way, is really only one way of using stories in coaching. Another way is to examine the stories our clients are telling *us*.

The truth is that we all tell stories. In fact, we tell stories of how we experience life. For example, you tell stories about where you've been the day before, where you're going out for dinner, how you got to where you are right now, what bus you took in the morning, or what happened when you drove your car that day. These are the stories we tell that describe our experiences. In fact, they *define* our experiences.

In essence, we define our life through the stories we tell. Sometimes those stories are not great stories; they are stories that don't serve us very well, yet they're completely and utterly subjective. We choose the characters, we choose the narrative, we choose the words that we use, and sometimes these stories create or define our reality in a way that doesn't do us good, and it keeps us in a very stuck place.

What I do with my clients—and what I teach other coaches to do with their clients—is I begin to examine the stories that my clients are telling, and look at how they can view the stories from different perspectives to create stronger, better, and more empowering stories. This helps them to shift the things they're feeling stuck in and to create a reality that's much more in line with their goals and the reality they want to create for themselves.

I: I have one client who doesn't hear me unless I give her an example.

LB: That's true for so many people. It's often difficult to deal with issues head on, but when we hear a story about someone else, it becomes much safer to take in the message. That person in the story is much more recognizable as we allow ourselves to play with and discover the story.

I: I was surprised to hear that you use storytelling for marketing and as a business tool. Can you elaborate on that?

LB: Absolutely. There are a couple of sides to the idea of using storytelling as a business tool. One aspect I think is really important is to use our own compelling story of who we are and how we came to offer the services we provide. Just developing and creating that story causes us to hone in on our niche and who our target market is. Discovering our compelling story is, in itself, the process we need to go through to determine our niche. Then, when we start using that story, it becomes an incredibly strong client-attraction tool.

It's almost like an elevator speech, although I'm not a fan of elevator speeches in general because they become too practiced and then they don't have any life left. But if you can be prepared to tell a story at a chance meeting with someone, what you say during those thirty seconds or two minutes that you have to make an impression becomes so much more compelling, and you attract clients much more easily.

Part of the work I do is to help people develop their own story so that they can use it to attract clients. When attracting clients, it is vital that you be very clear in regards to who your target market is and that you be tuned in to the narrative aspect of what you do and what service you offer your clients. It's a very powerful way to build your business. That's one side of using stories as a business-building tool.

The other side involves creating a safe space, building trust, and developing your listening skills. These are all the things you do when you learn how to become a story coach and to use storytelling in coaching. You're creating phenomenally powerful coaching skills.

The program I run is based on the ICF Core Competencies, and it's really about asking one's self, "How do I become a better coach and a more compelling coach?" Because at the end of the day, people love to hear stories, and stories sell. Stories sell *you* and they sell what you *do*, so when you start using storytelling in your coaching practice, it automatically becomes a powerful business tool for you.

> *"My vision is that everyone will understand how powerful this tool is and how incredibly compelling and influential stories can be."*

I: These sound like great coaching skills, but how does it actually build your business?

LB: A lot of coaches struggle with attracting clients and building their clientele. Through storytelling and story listening, you're offering such a compelling service that you differentiate yourself in the market.

The market is flooded—at least that is my sense. A lot of people call themselves coaches no matter how much experience or education they've had. Perhaps they read a book or put a sign on the door or have twenty-five years of experience coaching. The point is, you have to decide how to differentiate yourself. What's the story you're telling about yourself that sets you apart and makes you stand out in your market so that you attract clients and build your business?

As you actively listen through this narrative listening or story listening, you begin to understand your clients' needs in a very different way. In a sense, that defines your sales process. You become much more in tune with your clients' needs and can better provide what they want.

My vision is that everyone will understand how powerful this tool is and how incredibly compelling and influential stories can be, and that they will use this tool in their business. I'm so excited about it, and I love the idea that there could be lots of story coaches out there. People hear the term *story coach* and they wonder, *What is that, and how do I become a story coach?*

I believe we are all storytellers and that anyone can learn how to find their own story as well as other stories that are out there and use them as part of their coaching process. Storytelling is an integral part of coaching, but not everyone realizes that yet. A lot of the skills that are needed to use storytelling in a holistic, empowered, and powerful way within coaching are skills that can be acquired if they don't already exist.

So many people naturally tell wonderful stories. Coaches love to listen and love to talk; that's part of why we do what we do, so I think storytelling comes naturally to a lot of coaches. Several of the coaches that have come through my Certified Story Coach Program are perfect examples of these natural storytellers I'm referring to. I'm amazed after their first or second meeting when they come out with these incredible stories. I say, "Wow! It's so right that you should be here, because you tell wonderful stories." In my experience, most people, once they are given a few guidelines, are able to tell amazing stories; it's about acquiring the right skills and then honing them.

"I believe we are all storytellers and that anyone can learn how to find their own story . . . Storytelling is an integral part of coaching . . . I see these stories as a gift, both to me and to my clients."

I: Can you give us an example of a specific coaching scenario when storytelling made a difference?

LB: Sure. I have lots of examples of people who have been either starting a coaching business or in the middle of building up a business they've been in for some years when they discovered their story by going through this process. It first looks at discovering the story, then creating the story, and then looking at the ways that you actually present it. It's a real step-by-step process.

One particular client said to me, "It was amazing. It was so much more than just the story; it was like a reclaiming, a renaming, or a re-envisioning of who I am." We could connect to things that had been there forever, but she had never really looked at them in terms of who she is right now, and that is what the story process does.

Once she had defined that and created her story, she became much more focused on who she was offering her services to. This was not a brand new coach. She had been in the business for quite a while. But it suddenly became clear that she wanted to continue to work with a certain area of her clientele, and that, in regards to another area that she *had* been working with, she was no longer in that space anymore. By discovering her story, this all became clear for her. I see these stories as a gift, both to me and to my clients.

Chapter
12

Serve People—Make an Impact on the World
Michael Charest

Chapter 12
Serve People—Make an Impact on the World
Michael Charest

Michael is a twelve-year veteran business coach, consultant, author, and speaker. He is President of Business Growth Solutions, a company that specializes in helping solo and micro businesses attract more clients, grow their business, and live the prosperous life they deserve. To date, thousands of business owners have grown as a result of Michael's live seminars, teleprograms, audio products, books, and workbooks.

Michael held senior management positions with both Embassy Suites and American Golf Corporation, then founded two successful companies: Coach and Grow Rich and Business Growth Solutions. He understands firsthand the struggles of the small business owner.

Michael's current speaking program allows him to share his knowledge and experience in starting a business and surviving in business as well as how to sell and market yourself and your products in a successful, nonstressful, and fun way.

In addition to training and speaking, Michael wrote and published *From Grunt to Greatness: A Different Kind of Self-Help Book* in October 2005, a humorous but hard-hitting lesson on loving ourselves now and enjoying the journey as we pursue our personal best.

Michael's passion is writing and speaking. He travels throughout the United States and internationally, delivering high-energy, educational, inspirational, and humorous talks.

I: What inspires you, Michael?

MC: I'm a pretty passionate guy, so I get inspired by a lot of things, but the thing I most love doing and that I'm most inspired by is helping people reach their goals.

I grew up listening to self-help audios, going to see great speakers, reading great books, and as a kid I used to think, *Wow! What must it be like to be able to do that for a living?* Those speakers and authors inspired me so much. I got the bug to not only be inspired, but to inspire.

I try to live my life inspiring others, and for me it's not about being perfect and living "the perfect life." My book is titled *From Grunt to Greatness.* I'm kind of a grunt. I'm a workhorse. I'm a regular guy who has struggles and challenges just like everyone else, but I'm inspired to pursue my personal best, to achieve my goals, and to reach my dreams; the way I do that is by helping others. The coolest thing about our business is that we get to practice what we preach. That's what inspires me.

I: How do you inspire others?

MC: A lot of it happens through humor. One of my main messages is that you can do it; you *can* achieve the life of your dreams. My teaching is about helping others understand that you can have the business of your dreams, and part of that is about believing you can do it. Believe in yourself, believe in your products and services, and believe in your ability to market.

I strive to inspire people to believe, and I do that through speaking, writing, blogs, the Internet, and teleclasses; it's all about helping others believe they can do it.

I believe God put us here for a reason and that these goals and dreams we have within us are not there by accident; God put them in our hearts. Part of my mission on earth is to help bring that forth. Don't get me wrong, God does that, but I try to be a vehicle and to do it with humor.

We have a tendency to ask ourselves, "Who am I to want to be a millionaire, or a successful business owner, or to attract my soul mate, or to have a great house, or to be a great parent? Who am I to live this life?" We all deserve it. We all have our struggles and our challenges. I try to inspire others using humor—by poking fun at myself while sharing my struggles—and people get a kick out of it. They think, *Well, if Mike can do it with all the mistakes he's made, then maybe I can too.*

I: Do you have a story you can share that would serve as an example of what you're talking about?

MC: I'm sure I have many, but one of the stories I tell in my book took place about thirteen years ago. After years of wanting to be a life coach and a business coach (back in the early days I wanted to be a life coach), I attended a Peter Lowe seminar at the LA Forum and there must have been twenty thousand people there. Zig Zigler was speaking there as well as Colin Powell and maybe Tony Robbins.

I thought, *Wow, anyone who would go to a Peter Lowe seminar is in my market.* So I created a flyer. There was no way I could have gotten it on twenty thousand cars, so I hired a group of six people to help me place three thousand flyers on the windshields of the cars there, while avoiding the security guards because you're not supposed to do that. It was pouring rain, so we had to go to the store and buy plastic bags to put each flyer in.

I had an 800 number listed on the flyer. I thought, *There are three thousand people here. Even if only 1% of the people respond, I'm going to get thirty clients just from this one marketing strategy. I'm going to be full by the end of the day.* I rushed home. I couldn't wait to see how many messages I had—which was zero. I got two calls over the next three weeks, and I gained zero clients.

Once I tell people that, they say, "Oh, you did that? Wait until you hear what I did! Wait until you hear how I fell flat on *my* face!"

What do we do? We have to get up and shake ourselves off. We have a tendency to think that some of the big players out there—the people we admire—didn't struggle, and of course they did.

I: You mentioned Anthony Robbins. He talks about how he fell on his face as well and had trouble when he started out.

MC: Isn't that great? One of the things we love about Tony Robbins is that he's this big handsome guy, and he's so massive in his success, but he keeps it real.
I: You sort of answered this, but why did you choose this arena for

your life's great work?

MC: Throughout my life I studied self-help, and I always thought, *Maybe someday I could do something like that.* I also had a dream to be a hotel manager. I used to watch the show *Hotel.* I would look at James Brolin—who played the general manager of the hotel—and the fact that he drove a Porsche. I thought, *Oh wow, that's the life!* I literally chose the hotel industry because of that, while tempering my desire to be in the self-help field.

I did the hotel thing and then finally said, "You know what? I'm going to do this." I didn't know what "this" was called, but I found a book, *The Portable Coach,* by Thomas Leonard. I devoured that book in a Barnes and Noble one day, bought it, and went home and registered for a coaching skills weekend with Coach U. That's how it all started for me.

Over the first couple of years, I began honing my focus toward helping service professionals, because I believe service professionals—people who start their own business—are the coolest people in the world. They've had the courage to leave Corporate America to pursue their dream, and yet they struggle. I started saying, "These are the people I want to help, in large part because they're me."

When I first started my coaching business I was so sure I was going to be successful that I rented a condo for $2,500 a month. It was on the beach in Southern California. I was so close to the water that I could hear the whales. After month two, I couldn't make my rent payment and experienced many tough months and even years. I said, "This is the group of people I want to help because they're like me, and like me, they deserve to have success, but they don't know how to do it." That's how it came full circle.

From there, my focus evolved to being a service-based professional coach to teach individuals sales and marketing. That's kind of wrapped in the overall self-help umbrella, but along the way I found that there are a number of areas where service-based professionals fall flat in regards to marketing their businesses.

Success in business is a science, meaning you can follow certain steps, certain laws. Of course there are laws of the universe, such as the Law of Gravity, the Law of Reciprocity, and the Law of Attraction, but I'm talking about laws for converting a prospect from a place of interest to becoming a buyer. There are eleven specific steps to walk them through in order to accomplish this.

As service providers, we owe it to ourselves to learn what we need to learn in order to get leads, to cultivate those leads, and to turn those leads into clients. It's a science with an artistic flair; you, as the service provider, can put your own personal brand on it, but you can't ignore the steps.

Solopreneurs get into trouble because they want to create everything on their own. They think it's almost wrong to find out what the model is and to copy it. Don't reinvent the wheel. There is a science behind it and a system already in place. Follow the system, put your personal touch on it—that's where the art comes in—and then do it.

So many people don't take action. To make a quarter of a million dollars a year as a service professional, you need to be spending 25% of your work time marketing, which is twelve and a half hours a week or fifty hours a month.

"Success is the pursuit of your personal best, without attachment to outcome, while enjoying the journey along the way."

When I say teach this to people, they nearly fall out of their chairs. They say, "I'm not spending anywhere near that amount of time!" I respond, in a loving way of course, "Well, that's why you're not bringing in anywhere near a quarter of a million dollars. If you follow this system, stick to the steps, apply yourself, and learn what to do and how to do it, you will achieve success. It's indisputable." Any client I've ever coached who followed this system and took action got tremendous results. It's not rocket science, just follow the steps.

I: How do you define success?

MC: I have spent an enormous amount of time thinking about how to define success, and it's what my book is about. To me, success is the pursuit of your personal best, without attachment to outcome, while enjoying the journey along the way. Let me break that down.

Success is the *pursuit,* not necessarily the *attainment,* of your personal best. You may never attain that which God made you capable of attaining, but I think success is found in the pursuit of it.

We owe it to ourselves to pursue it and to enjoy the journey along the way.

Another piece I add is the pursuit of success in each critical element of life, which includes money, family, relationships, our career, our health, etc. Success is that pursuit; whether or not we attain it, what matters is that we're giving it our all and we're enjoying it along the way.

I: I agree, because what success means to me may be completely different from what it means to you. It can't just be about money or a relationship for everyone. You can't define someone else's success.

MC: No, and it's funny that you say that because another way you can define success is as whatever *you* think it is. That's really all that matters. If you define it one way and I define it another, as long as we've got our own solid definition and we're going for it, that's success.

I: What is your most powerful moment of success or life change?

MC: I don't know that I can define my most powerful moment of success, but I think what I am most proud of—and I use that term loosely—is having the courage to leave Corporate America to start my own business, and then to create and manage that in an ethical way that supports my family.

I'm not married, but one of the things I said when I started my business was that if my mom, my sister-in-law, and my brother want to work with me, they can. I wanted to provide a stay-at-home environment for my family. My dad was sick at the time and he has since died, that's why I didn't mention him. Well, he would never want to work for me, and I mean that in a good way.

To this day I am proud to say that my mom and my sister-in-law both work for me full time and my brother works for me part time; we've really created a family business. That and just the fact that I took the risk of starting this—that which I felt I was put on earth to do— and had the courage to do it, because it was really hard; that makes me feel successful.

I: It does take a lot of courage to step out on your own. You mentioned that it's difficult, but what would you recommend that would possibly make it easier? This whole process creates fear in a lot of people, so what is something you went through that you could recommend to help someone who really wants to step out, but hasn't taken that step yet?

MC: There are so many different levels, but I think the first one is to pray. For those reading this, I pray that you know that the feeling you have within, the stirring that you have, is from a higher power. Just trust that that's not you. You're not longing to make a leap because *you* want it. God is placing that within you. Find peace and know that you're not alone. There are coaches and people out there who can support you, but it all starts with God. That feeling you have is coming from your Creator. What a good feeling!

Commit to taking a step. Maybe it's a tiny step each day or a little bit bigger step each week. You might say, "I'm going to read something inspirational every day for the next week," or "I'm going to pray." A bigger step might be committing once a week, "I'm going to research a coach who might be able to help me," or "I'm going to Google this topic—this profession that I think I might want to take a leap in pursuing—and I'm going to do some research."

What happens is this higher power starts leading you and putting the right people and the right things in your path. The next step is to simply pay attention. Realize what's happening. You'll see signs, you'll meet people, and you'll find things to read and Web sites that seemingly flow to you. Pay attention and commit to taking another step. And all the while remember you're being guided. I kept saying that to myself: "There's a reason I'm being pulled to not want to be a country club manager anymore. God has something bigger in store, and I owe it to myself and to Him to pursue that."

I: I talk to a lot of different people who are at various levels of success, but I'll tell you, every one of them—the ones that have stepped out on their own—have the same consistent thought: they didn't choose this for their life's work, it was chosen for them. They were called to do exactly this, and all the successful people I know have that calling, that feeling. They didn't choose it, it chose them.

MC: I appreciate you saying that, because I know you've interviewed a lot of incredible people, and just hearing you validate something I said as a result of your personal experience and what you've heard from other people is awesome.
I heard Jack Canfield say something once about how the headlight of a car only shines two hundred feet ahead. You don't need to see the

light illuminating from New York City to Providence, Rhode Island in order to get there. You just need to see the two hundred feet in front of you. Then, as you move forward, the light goes another two hundred feet from that point. I've never forgotten that. I thought, *Wow, that's perfect!* You'll make yourself sick trying to figure it all out in advance and asking yourself, "How am I going to make the jump? Where am I going to get the money? What is my wife going to think? What happens if I fail? How am I going to create a Web site?" Just focus on the next step.

I: Like you said, it will flow to you. If you don't go the way you're supposed to go, life will push you there eventually. Then, once you're on your right path, like you said, it flows to you. It comes to you, and doors will open that you didn't even know were there. You're able to see opportunities that you had no idea existed.

MC: There's one thing I want to say that goes along with that; I don't know if this is the same as or different from what other people say, but I need to speak my truth. Even with all that, it's not easy. For those who are reading this and thinking, *Oh, so he's saying that leaving my career and starting my own business will be easy.* No way am I saying that!

Something being easy and something being the right thing are two different things entirely. I hope that doesn't come off as sounding cynical, but rather as real, so that when you encounter five hundred road blocks and you fall and you get back up, you're not thinking, *Oh, I'm the only one. Mike and these other folks said it was going to be easy. There must be something wrong.* No, I'm not saying it's easy, but you've got to do it anyway.

I: What are the three most important personal tips you could share for achievement and fulfillment?

Three Tips for Finding Achievement and Fulfillment

1. Work on building your belief on a daily basis. Take time out of every single day—I beg you—to build your personal belief in yourself. I think a lack of self-esteem and a lack of self-love—or maybe it's cracks in our armor of self-love and acceptance—are what get in our way most often.

Read inspirational material. Repeat your mantras. Practice visualizations. Say your prayers or your incantations. Go for power walks. It's not rocket science and you've got to do it. Thirty minutes in the morning and thirty minutes at night—that's all it takes.

The first thing I do when I wake up in the morning is I say, "I love myself, I love myself, I love myself. I can do it. I'm special. God put me here for a reason." Repeat those kinds of mantras. That's number one.

2. Take action. Everyone has great ideas. Everyone has plans. The difference between those who make it and those who don't are the ones who act—period. It sounds simple. We've heard Tony Robbins say it nine billion times: take action—take massive action.

The only difference between the ones who are thinking about it and the ones who are doing it is action. What makes us act? Belief. If you see someone taking action, they believe in themselves. If you see someone hiding, they don't.

3. Measure your results. Believe, take action, and then measure. Is it working? Is it working well? What kinds of results are other people getting? How are your results better or worse than theirs? What could you be doing to do better?

"It's not about the pursuit of success for the sake of success, but rather for the sake of serving people—to make an impact on the world. What else is there?"

Those are three things we continually teach in our program. If you believe in yourself, take action, measure the results, and then fine tune and never stop committing to improvement, it becomes a life cycle; it never ends, and you'll always be growing.

You want to talk about enjoying the journey—it's fun. Growth is fun. The pursuit of success is fun. That's what I believe it's all about. It's not about the pursuit of success for the sake of success, but rather for the sake of serving people—to make an impact on the world. What else is there?

I: That being said, you're never working, you're just enjoying yourself.

MC: There are days when I definitely feel like I'm working, but for the most part, I can't tell between work and play. Not long ago I hosted a seminar at my house. We conducted a speaking mastery.

Eight people attended. My mom came and we cooked them breakfast, lunch, and dinner. We played with the dog, we got in the hot tub, and we worked our butts off in front of a camera. People were learning how to speak and how to sell from the podium. Is that work or play? Does that sound like work? Not to me.

I: You talked about building belief as it applies to you—tell me how your other two tips work for you.

MC: As far as action, I'm a big believer—and I alluded to this earlier—that there's a science happening here. For example, I map out a monthly plan for my clients. There are certain things you should be doing every day, every week, and every month in order to achieve the success you desire. For me, it's a matter of committing to that and using my coach to hold me accountable.

I'm just like everyone else. If I'm not held accountable, I'll find anything else to do other than what I committed to doing. It's a funny thing, and we don't have time to get into the psychology of it. Even if we did, I don't know that I know the answer. But we don't do what we know we need to do. It's important to have someone to hold you accountable. I commit to my coach, "These are the twenty-two things I'm going to do this week to move my business and my life forward." During our next call, he'll ask me, "Did you do this?" That's action.

As far as measuring results goes, I've done a lot of research in this area. I'm always creating thresholds. For every action, there is a goal and a measurement. Did I achieve it, or didn't I? Did I get the results, or didn't I? Then I scrutinize. I ask myself, "What could I have done better?" That's how it works. It's a bit laborious, but you get into a pattern where everything you're doing is action, measurement, fine tuning, action, measurement, fine tuning.

I do a lot of that with my coach, and that's the work I do for other people too, because God bless us, we don't take action if we don't have a coach kicking us, inspiring us, and cajoling us along the way.

The following books were referenced by our experts within their interviews. Some are written by these experts themselves, and some are books that have impacted their life or business.

Awakening the Entrepreneur Within by Michael E. Gerber
Banker to the Poor by Muhammad Yunus
Brilliance Unbridled by Kendall SummerHawk
Chicken Soup for the Soul Series by multiple authors
Frankenstein by Mary Shelley
From Grunt to Greatness: A Different Kind of Self-Help Book by Michael Charest
Global Leadership: The Next Generation by Marshall Goldsmith, Dr. Cathy Greenberg, Alastair Robertson, Maya Hu-Chan
Harry Potter Series by J.K. Rowling
How to Quickly Get Started in Professional Coaching: The Truth About What it Really Takes by Christian Mickelsen
Jane Eyre by Charlotte Bronte
Mojo by Marshall Goldsmith
Power vs Force by David R. Hawkins
Step Into the Spotlight: A Guide to Getting Noticed by Tsufit
Stranger in a Strange Land by Robert A. Heinlein
The E-Myth Enterprise by Michael E. Gerber
The E-Myth Revisited by Michael E. Gerber
The Fifth Agreement by don Miguel Ruiz, don Jose Ruiz, Janet Mills
The Four Agreements by don Miguel Ruiz
The Law of Abundance by Dr. Sherry Buffington
The Mastery of Love by don Miguel Ruiz
The Most Successful Small Business in the World by Michael E. Gerber
The Voice of Knowledge by don Miguel Ruiz, Janet Mills, Peter Coyote
Way of the Peaceful Warrior by Dan Millman
What Got You Here Won't Get You There by Marshall Goldsmith, Mark Reiter
What Happy Companies Know by Dr. Cathy Greenberg, Dan Baker, Collins Hemingway
What Happy Women Know by Dr. Cathy Greenberg, Dan Baker, Ina Yalof
What Happy Working Mothers Know by Dr. Cathy Greenberg, Barrett Avigdor

Michael E. Gerber
Best-Selling Author of *E Myth*, Transforming the
World One Business at a Time
www.michaelegerber.com

Dr. Cathy Greenberg
NY Times Best-Selling Author, Global Thought
Leader in Organizational Development
www.xcelinstitute.com
www.h2cleadership.com

Dr. Relly Nadler
International Leadership Expert, Author, and World-
Class Executive Coach
www.xcelinstitute.com
www.truenorthleadership.com

Kendall SummerHawk
Million Dollar Marketing Coach, Author, Speaker,
Mentor
www.iawbc.org/pg/joiniawbc.html#register

Christian Mickelsen
Author of *How to Quickly Get Started in
Professional Coaching*
www.coacheswithclients.com

Dr. Sherry Buffington
Psychologist, Coach, Trainer, Author of *The Law Of
Abundance*
www.sherrybuffington.com

Viki Winterton
Network and Publishing Expert, International Change Agent to Fortune 100 Teams, Founder of Expert Insights Family of Opportunity
www.getei.com

Tsufit
Coaching Dynamo, Former Attorney, Acclaimed Author of *Step Into the Spotlight: A Guide to Getting Noticed*
www.tsufit.com

James Malinchak
Consummate Speaker of the Year, Author, Coach, Featured on the ABC's Hit Series *Secret Millionaire*
www.malinchak.com

Dr. Sharon Melnick
Psychologist, Coach, Harvard Researcher Helping Talented and Successful People Get Out of Their Own Way
www.sharonmelnick.com

Lisa Bloom
Founder of Story Coach, Inc. and the ICF Accredited Story Coach Certification Program
www.lisabloom.com

Michael Charest
Author, Speaker, Small Business Mentor, President of Business Growth Solutions
www.bgsllc.com

Abundance Audit Assessment
How would you assess yourself in key areas for applying an appreciation for abundance in your professional and personal life? Find out now!
www.h2cleadership.com/resources/tools.shtml

Are You Talented But Getting in Your Own Way?
Receive the free webinar *Confidence at the Core: 3 Steps to Own the Room, Earn What You Are Worth, and Ensure Your Hard Work Leads to Success.* Get Ready to land your biggest client ever, have the confidence to be effective and respected in your position. and have ease and power in your personal relationships.
www.sharonmelnick.com

Business Growth Solutions
Business Growth Solutions developed a comprehensive, step-by-step business building system that has helped thousands of clients become more successful. If you sell a service, we can help you. Schedule a complimentary consultation to take your business to the next level!
www.bgsllc.com/about/index.htm

CORE Gets Right to the Heart of What Really Matters
With CORE, analysis of natural and conditioned traits, development levels of essential competencies, emotional intelligence, coping patterns, and which behaviors create stress and which motivate and energize are all presented in one unified system. Take your CORE profile.
www.coremap.com/index.php/core-profile.html

Entrepreneurship is the Next Big Thing
But only Michael E. Gerber knows what you can do about it. Visit a place where original thinking is held at a premium, passion is the key to admission, and entrepreneurship is not just a word, but an action. Become a leader of the new entrepreneur movement in your community. LEAP IN and receive a free gift!
www.michaelegerber.com

Free Book From James Malinchak
For the last twelve years, James has been traveling around the world with his motivational speaking, helping people achieve their goals, and trying to make a difference in everyone's life. James invites you to get a FREE copy of his new book by visiting this link.
www.malinchak.com

Free Leadership Assessment
Assessments are designed to give you insights while the accompanying Action Plan helps you design a path forward. Take this step to better understand yourself and to increase your leadership skills.
www.truenorthleadership.com/assessments-opt-in

Money, Marketing, and Soul
Is the maverick in you ready for an easy, simple system to brand, package, and price your services so you can move away from "dollars-for-hours" work—fast—and create more money, time, and freedom in your business? Put the spirit of FREEDOM back into doing what you love! FREE audio interview: *7 Simple Steps to Create Your Multiple Streams of Income "Money and Soul" Business*
www.kendallsummerhawk.com

Need Help to Attract the Spotlight?
11 Free Secrets From the Spotlight! Tips for how to stand out and get noticed every time you open your mouth in public!
www.tsufit.com/blog/11-free-secrets-of-the-spotlight/

Want More Clients in the Next 7 Days?
Get a rush of new clients this week using these free tools. You'll be able to attract clients FAST. In fact ,you'll be able to cause a rush of new business on demand any time you want as well as find people that want to hire you so you can scoop up new clients everywhere you go. Get 5-15 new clients this week—or even right now today—by putting these three tools into action immediately. (And it only takes a few minutes to do!)
www.coacheswithclients.com

Write Away, Write Now!
Whether you write for your own enjoyment, need marketing copy for your products and services, are an experienced author, publisher, or speaker, or are just beginning the idea stage of your book, you'll find what you need here! Receive FREE access to our global writers' community and 6-week Journaling Program!
www.writeawaywritenow.com

Your Story Is Your Success
Entrepreneurs de-stress the marketing and build their business with confidence and balance by finding their success story. Free e-book, *Using Stories to Get Great Clients.*
www.story-coach.com

Home of Best-selling, Award-winning Books

Best Seller
amazon.com

eLit Awards

Ready,
Aim,
Impact!

The Exper[...]
for Entre[...]

For[...]
Best-Selling[...]

Best Seller
amazon.com

eLit Awards
Gold Medal

Ready,
Aim,
Excel!

The Expert
Weekly Guide
and Professiona[...]

Featur[...]
Drs. Marshall Goldsmith[...]
Relly Nadler, Ke[...]
and 48 Top Leade[...]

Best Seller
amazon.com

Ready,
Aim,
Soar!

The [...]
for Bus[...]

Wounded?
Survive!
Thrive!!!

101 Women's Journeys from
Torment to Triumph

With a forward by NY Times Best Selling Author Dr. Cathy Greenberg

Ready,
Aim,
Captivate!

**Put Magic in Your Message and
a Fortune in Your Future.**

**Featuring Deepak Chopra, Ran Zilca,
Suzi Pomerantz, Dan Janal, and Jim Stovall**

Our mission is to give authors a voice and a platform on which to stand. We specialize in books covering innovative ways to meet the personal and business challenges of the 21st century.

Through our signature, inexpensive publishing, and marketing services, we help authors publish and promote their works more effectively and connect to readers in a uniquely efficient system.

We employ an experienced team of online marketing strategists, ad copywriters, graphic artists, and Web designers whose combined talents ensure beautiful books, effective online marketing campaigns at easily affordable rates, and personal attention to you and your needs.

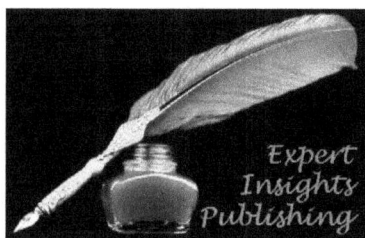

Would you like to be showcased with experts?

How do you get known and stand out as an expert in your market? The company you keep can position you, and your book can be your most powerful platform to:

⟶ provide you with maximum exposure,

⟶ reinforce your credentials, and

⟶ build your credibility.

Who Can Be a Co-Author?

This is your unique opportunity to share your personal and professional story and experiences with the world in your private interview, transcribed and published alongside global experts, visionaries, and best-selling authors. Lean more about our current publishing opportunities at www.ReadyAimPublish.com.

www.ingramcontent.com/pod-product-compliance
Lightning Source LLC
Chambersburg PA
CBHW072008090426
42740CB00011B/2141